Ageless Faith

Ageless Faith

A Conversation between Generations about Church

Keith Drury
and
David Drury

Compliments of...
wesleyan publishing house
P.O. Box 50434
Indianapolis, IN 46250-0434

Call: 800.493.7539 • Fax: 800.788.3535
E-mail: wph@wesleyan.org • Online: www.wesleyan.org/wph
Please send copies of any review or mention.

wesleyan
publishing
house

Indianapolis, Indiana

Copyright © 2010 by Keith Drury and David Drury
Published by Wesleyan Publishing House
Indianapolis, Indiana 46250
Printed in the United States of America
ISBN: 978-0-89827-404-2

Library of Congress Cataloging-in-Publication Data

Drury, Keith W.
    Ageless faith : a conversation between generations about church / Keith Drury and
David Drury.
        p. cm.
    ISBN 978-0-89827-404-2
    1. Wesleyan Church--Doctrines. 2. Intergenerational communication--Religious
aspects--Wesleyan Church. I. Drury, David. II. Title.
    BX9995.W45D78 2010
    230'.71--dc22
                                                    2009038767

Contents

Acknowledgements   7

Preface   9

1. Worship   13

2. Conversion   25

3. Community   41

4. Race   53

5. Heaven   63

6. Alcohol   73

7. Sanctification   87

8. Women in Leadership   101

9. Denominational Leadership   111

10. Ordained Ministry   123

11. Intergenerational Dialogue   137

Teacher Tips   147

Acknowledgements

This book is all about conversation and interaction. Can we thank those whose conversations with us have helped us most?

Keith would like to thank . . .

Sharon Drury–thanks for the steady surety of your own personal faith and your own interest in the next generation . . . you inspire me!

David and John Drury–thanks for the many hours we've spent talking our way through these and other things as we drove around Turkey or Austria or went backpacking in the high Sierras or ate too much over the holidays. Your insights have helped me understand the younger generation far more than reading this book will ever help anyone else. You are beloved sons in whom I am well pleased.

My colleagues–thank you especially to David Smith, Ken Schenck, Russ Gunsalus, Burt Webb, Kris Pence, Chris Bounds, Charlie Alcock, and the many other professors who sharpen my thinking every day through the school year—but especially on Fridays when we eat together.

My students–thank you for the many conversations you give me over coffee, in my office, and as we've hiked and cycled together. I believe deeply in your generation, and your frank and open discussions with me have been instructive and are always encouraging to me.

David would like to thank . . .

Keith Drury—as always with you, Dad, the conversation has been interesting! You are a great writer and teacher, but most don't know you are an even better father and grandpa.

Steve DeNeff—your vision for the Church is bigger than anything I have heard, short of the dreams of Christ in John 17. Thanks for sowing that seed in my own soul each Sunday.

Max Lucado—as an author you are peerless. Somehow, in your love of the Church, you still treat all as your peers. I hope that rubs off on me more.

Maxim, Karina, and Lauren Drury—God grants me joy daily through you. I hope the church you inherit from us is ready to go to the next level. You deserve it.

Kathy Drury—in this book we have discussed an ageless *faith*. Thank you for believing in it and me. For you I have an ageless *love*.

Keith and David would like to thank . . .

Jim Wood—you have one of the sharper minds around and we thank you for using your iron to sharpen ours in the manuscript.

Don Cady, Kevin Scott, and the WPH Team—thank you for your vision behind this book and for shepherding it *and* us through the process.

Preface

Each new generation inherits the church from the previous one and tries to change it for the better. When the older generations of today inherited the church, they made substantial changes. Now younger generations are emerging who have their own changes in mind. This book is about those changes.

It is a discussion between a boomer in his sixties (Keith) and a member of the younger generation in his thirties (David). They also happen to be father and son. Keith Drury represents the older generation—boomers and those above. David Drury represents the emerging generations, those in their twenties and thirties. Those in their forties can often go either way; in some churches, they *are* the younger generation. We'd like to offer a few notes of explanation before we begin the conversation.

We Invite You to Look Over Our Shoulders

This book comes from the Wesleyan "tribe." We are Wesleyan ministers writing about issues that repeatedly come up in Wesleyan circles. However, the issues we raise frequently come up in other denominations as well, like the Nazarenes and Free Methodists and tribes of all other shapes, sizes, and styles. This book is an invitation for you to look over our shoulders, to gain insight from our experiences in this particular context, and to apply those insights in your own setting and circumstances.

We Sometimes Play a Role

To fairly represent our generations, we sometimes exaggerate our positions a bit; thus, our personal differences may appear greater than they really are. Keith is less of an old fogy and David less of a rebel than we might appear to be in this book. Both sides need to be heard, and so we're ensuring the opinions here are forceful—not just "straw men."

We Hope Generations Will Study This Book Together

Our hope is that generations will come together for a few months to read and discuss this book. We've designed discussion questions for each issue to open thoughtful dialogue between generations in each local church. We think the generations can find common ground through these conversations. This book could be studied by one generation alone in a class or group, but if you do that, beware of taking the ain't-it-awful one-sided approach and identifying with only your own generation's side in the discussion. Refer to the Teacher Tips at the end of this book for help leading discussion.

Generational Generalizations Are Never Absolute

While we represent broad differences between generations, there are limits to such generalizations, and you'll find plenty of exceptions. As an older person, you might identify more with David's position at times, and younger folk will sometimes find themselves more in line with Keith's positions. No generalization can represent all the people of a generation. However, these concerns are hot issues of the day and worthy of serious and thoughtful discussion in order to find the way forward for the church.

Our Discussion Was Enlightening to Us—We Hope the Same for You

This book grew out of dozens of father-son chats. We have our differences, but we have found a lot of agreement too. We have moved toward each other through our discussions, because we both love the Church and have dreams for God's kingdom that include each other's generations (and are impossible without them). We hope the generations will talk together to find greater unity and strength. The leadership of the church will soon pass to a new generation. It's just a matter of time. Thoughtful talk between generations makes a stronger, more unified church for the future. We need each other! While our approaches may vary and our emphases differ, we must find common ground because the core faith we hold is ageless.

—Keith Drury, July 2009
—David Drury, July 2009

1

Worship

Why don't we sing the old hymns anymore?
Why are the older people in this church always complaining about the music?
If people don't like the worship, there are plenty of other churches to go to.
Is the organ our idol—the golden calf of our sanctuary?
I haven't felt the Spirit move in any of these new songs.
Why does the music have to be so loud?
Everyone here likes the music just the way it is.
Do we have to have drums and guitars cluttering up the sacred chancel?
Why are we still having "worship wars"—can't we all just get along?

KEITH: Why is the latest worship music such a downer? It seems like the tone is somber and sad, instead of bright and joyful. Many of us boomers think Christians should be upbeat and peppy in worship instead of singing forlornly in a way that might sound to outsiders like we are mourning our religion rather than celebrating it. That's one of the reasons we boomers made the transition from hymns to choruses.

DAVID: I can see why you might think that our music is a downer compared to the music boomers prefer. Younger people today are very sensitive to the need for authenticity. This is a reaction against what many see as the fake-feeling, up-front leadership of boomers. I admit that we often go to the other extreme. Even when our lyrics signal hope, the tone can feel more like the book of Ecclesiastes or Job.

You are used to a happy-clappy boomer style of music—the "We Bring the Sacrifice of Praise" genre. However, there is a long tradition of more mournful music in the church. We're just highlighting that part of the canon of church music—the part that got lost in the boomer praise shuffle the last half-century.

KEITH: True, we boomers didn't much like the downer music of the past. Maybe it is OK to bring some back now, so long as you don't make *all* the music mournful.

But, here's another thing. Why do many younger folk want it so dark in the sanctuary? It reminds me of those old churches we boomers took over forty years ago—dim, dank, dark, and dismal. They were depressing! We brightened up the place, spiced up the atmosphere, made it more cheerful, and added spotlights to brighten up the stage. Now you guys come along turning off the lights and sticking candles everywhere. How come? It seems to us like a step backward.

DAVID: This reflects the move of the younger generation from presentation to participation, from stage to congregation. Multi-sensory worship helps us connect with one another and with God. We think it feels more authentic instead of the stage showmanship we are tired of. A spotlight on a singer holding an orange foam-covered mike performing for the audience doesn't feel authentic to us. When we attend a concert, we expect a concert; when we come to worship, we expect worship. Dim lights and candles are our attempt to take performance off the stage to create a subdued, holy, and reverent atmosphere. We're weary of watching worship.

KEITH: OK, we dumped the foam mike covers by the end of the 80's, but I admit we boomers did focus more attention on the stage (what our parents called the platform). It seems to us that you guys don't want any attention on the leader at all; everything is so understated. We were raised with a song leader and we introduced a praise team instead. You guys seem to want even less showmanship than that—we hardly know who's in charge. That may be OK; perhaps we've gone too far in making worship something to watch.

But, here's another thing: Why do younger worship leaders have such affection for new songs? They act as if anything written more than ten years ago is ghastly. We have hundreds of years of good songs to sing. Why narrow down the selection to those from the last ten years, songs so few of us know?

DAVID: Yes, I'll confess that we younger folk think something *newer* is probably *better*. But we're not the first generation to think that. The old holiness folk dumped almost all the classic hymns and sang mostly holiness songs (the songs you now call "hymns").

We think there's energy in the lyrics and music written more recently. Songs are like testimonies; the more recent, the better. New "great hymns of the faith" should be written in every generation. Some younger worship leaders rearrange old hymns with new music to recapture the great words. Plus, some of the more popular worship songs these days are from oft-missed biblical passages. What about the song "Days of Elijah" or "You Have Done Great Things," which is from Psalm 126? That's old enough stuff, right?

KEITH: Sure, when new musicians use Scripture, few can complain. However, you brought up something I want to ask about. Why do worship leaders feel compelled to change the tunes of old songs, as if the original tune was obviously flawed and their new twist is such an improvement?

DAVID: Think of it as a translation. Many songs were written with a music style that wonderfully matched the musical language of the time. When new musical formats emerge, we can translate old lyrics into new tunes, and that refreshes the timeless message. Some of your books have been translated into other languages. Were you offended when they used different words? Of course not. In fact, you've updated the language in some of your books as the times changed. You didn't say, "Those people need to learn my language if they want to read my books." You changed the language so that your new readers would get what you were trying to say. That's what these musicians are doing: updating the translation.

I think the legendary hymn-writers are being honored by younger generations who want to reintroduce their words to people with new tunes—even some new lyrics. Most folk today don't even know what a "bulwark never failing" means. Besides, many hymn-writers didn't write the tunes of their songs; others set their words to music. We're just writing new tunes for old lyrics to translate the ideas into today's musical format. We can listen to music and know in less than a minute which decade it is from.

KEITH: Persuasive argument. You brought up *language*, and I think that's a good way to describe both lyrics and musical styles. That helps us see this whole discussion in a different light. The older generations speak a different native language in both style and lyrics. It seems to us, though, that the "musical missionaries" leading worship insist we learn their new language—so we worship just as they worshiped in their college chapels. When they do use our older native hymns they insist on changing them to their own language and expect us to learn their new language. They say all this is to adapt to the emerging culture, but sometimes we think they are merely making us adapt to their own taste preferences. We would never put up with missionaries making people learn a new language so they can truly worship better. How do younger worship leaders get away with this?

DAVID: That's a great point. This is where it gets complicated. Some churches are hiring the wrong worship leader if what they want is to keep their traditional music language. They should explore those issues in the interview. Of course, if our hearts are right, we also want to see younger generations and the unsaved in our worship too, so we have to make some compromises. This is where blended worship services come in, using a variety of music languages. However, I admit that transitioning to blended worship can be painful and sometimes, in the attempt to make everyone happy, we make everyone unhappy. Several of our younger worship leaders have caused problems by not being sensitive to the problem you're pointing out. They blindly assume "my way is the right way," which is just as wrong as an older person insisting on organ and hymns only. I suppose wrongheadedness about worship music is not limited to any one generation—young or old.

KEITH: When it comes to musical style there is lots of wrongheadedness to go around. Blended styles may be the best way to give everyone a little of what they prefer—sort of like having part of the service in Spanish, part in German, and part in English in a mixed congregation?

DAVID: Blenders make messy sandwiches. Something-for-everyone services often leave everyone missing something. That's why numerous churches have abandoned the blended service strategy and have started multiple venues and even video venues. Each venue offers a different musical language, just like some churches offer one service in English and a second service in Spanish or Mandarin.

KEITH: Separate venues might help in larger churches, but don't we pay a price when we do that too: isolating generations from one another?

DAVID: I was originally an opponent of multiple venues for that very reason, but over time, I have changed my mind. I've noticed many people's choice of venue would surprise you. In my last church, I was outside greeting people and a classy eighty-year-old lady pulled up into the handicapped spot by the curb. She wore a purple high-collared dress and walked with an ornate cane. When I discovered she was a visitor, I described our different venues, assuming she would choose our more traditional service in the sanctuary with pews and an organ. However, when I described our dimly lit rock-and-roll edgy worship service accompanied with flashing laser lights (what we called "59 West"), her eyes lit up and she said, "Oh, I'll try that one out—that sounds fun!"

KEITH: Who would have guessed?

DAVID: Not me, that's for sure. From that point on, I have stopped assuming generational tastes. My church's most traditional service in our sanctuary is actually our most multi-generational, and our liturgical service in a small chapel has no seniors at all and is made up mostly of college students and young adults. I was surprised to find out one of our young, trendy youth staff members goes to that liturgical venue by choice. On top of all this, I have begun to value the smaller communities that these venues and multiple services provide for people to connect with each other.

KEITH: You're right, maybe it isn't only about age but some people are simply more pliable than others. Still, average churches are usually limited to one service, so blending (or even picking one style) is about all they can do. Say, while we're praising pliability let me observe that I've noticed many young people are actually less pliable than older folk. The students I teach are more narrow-minded about musical styles than any old folk I know. They say, "I can't stand that kind of music" and refuse to even attend some services. Older folk may also say they hate the music, but at least they will attend and put up with it. Why can't younger folk be more pliable and accept traditional songs just as they expect older people to accept new songs?

DAVID: The students you have are the children of boomers. I think the problem you see isn't about music, but about consumerism. They were trained by their church-shopping parents to demand what suits their taste. You're right about the rigidity. They specify their worship in a similar way to ordering a *venti decaf soy fat free mocha latte* at Starbucks. Their tastes are narrow, and they expect the church to offer their exact preference in style. I agree this is a serious problem and worship venues aren't solving it. They may even be feeding this sort of consumerism. One of the things we are trying to do with our venue strategy is to learn from other venues. Our "interactive venue" keeps interaction in front of us, our "liturgical venue" keeps the value of the Lord's Supper in front of us, and our other venues help us remember newer or older styles too. We're finding that our experimental venues help teach the other venues.

KEITH: That's neat. One concern I have is that many older folk yearn for deep theological hymns and songs that are fortifying for when people go through difficult times. It seems that many of today's songs, while good at praise, have little to offer for Christian living. The lyrics often seem shallow.

DAVID: I think you might be talking about some of the songs we younger folk now consider "old." I'm not sure you can accuse the current music of shallowness like you could the '80s music. And even the older folk had plenty of shallow songs too. Here I'm thinking about the chirpy "Give Me Oil in My Lamp," and "Climb, Climb up Sunshine Mountain" choruses. These aren't very deep theologically, right? This is the very reason the emerging worship experience has those "dirge-like" new songs you mentioned. And it is why we have rescued old hymns with great truths re-fashioned and re-tuned—to help us grasp the depths of theology.

KEITH: I admit we had plenty of shallow choruses too. However, we also had "He Lives" or testimony songs like "The Longer I Serve Him" and songs chock full of theology like "How Firm a Foundation."

DAVID: We could do this all day. For every "Longer I Serve Him" you offer, I can toss back "Changed" by Aaron Niequist. For every "He Lives," I can offer you something like "God of Wonders." I'll see your "How Firm a Foundation" and raise you a "Gifted Response" and "God of the City." We must become the kind of church that creates room to raise up the next Fanny Crosby and Charles Wesley, rather than suppressing them by acting like those that lived two hundred years ago are the only ones who could write sound theological songs.

KEITH: I stand down—fair point. Maybe I am speaking of the shallow choruses we introduced in the '80s and '90s more than today's music. Perhaps I'm looking at "new music" as everything since 1980, and that's not your generation's fault. We boomers are the ones who led the shallow praise songs.

While we're speaking about singing, why do they make us stand so long while singing? Is standing the only way to sing? Some of the older folk above my generation have back problems, yet they want to cooperate so they stand and grimace through twenty minutes of singing. Why has standing become the required posture for singing?

DAVID: I'm not sure the length of the singing is anything different than you experienced when you were younger. Certainly it's shorter than the song services at those protracted camp meeting services I've heard about. You guys did twenty minutes of standing for altar calls, for goodness sake! Perhaps the songs are not getting longer; the backs are getting weaker? Today's more sensitive worship leaders do include sit-down breaks or even invite people to stand only if they want to. Ironically, in many of the interactive worship services, people routinely sit around tables during the singing and never stand at all—like they are at a jazz club.

KEITH: Sitting down while others are standing means something negative to many of us, so we don't want to do that "optional" sitting thing. To us sitting down while others are standing is like going on strike in our minds. Remember, we were raised with sit-ins and sit-down strikes.

DAVID: Of course, that would be reading too much into it today. My generation never experienced sit-down strikes. All kinds of physical postures can be used in worship and be pleasing to God. You're hinting at something that is important, however, and I'd like to hear what you think the older generations might say to younger worship leaders and pastors so we can be a better church for all generations in the future. What coaching would you give us from the older generation?

KEITH: Well, I probably already said most of it. We want younger folk to respect some of our native language at least a little. Not just by letting us sing some of our songs occasionally, begrudgingly tossing us a few verses just to pacify us, but by embracing them and singing them with *gusto*. All the older songs couldn't be completely useless. Making us stand is OK, but let us sit some of the time without making us look like we are feeble or like we are going on strike. Maybe sing a few uplifting songs occasionally—we need some uplift in our musical diet. And, maybe some of the youngsters could write some new testimony songs, especially songs we could quote or remember as we face difficulties or the death of our friends. We want to be team players, but we'd like a chance to have the ball occasionally. That's about it for us. We are team players and we won't leave the church over music. But, what about you? Representing emerging generations, what would you say to us older folk?

DAVID: I'm guessing that many in the older generations are just tired of this debate. Some have been arguing about this stuff for three decades and are either giving up or hanging on by a thread. I'd love to see some church leaders band together to take an honest and collaborative approach to this. Just fighting against the new and then eventually giving up is the worst approach. That results in too many casualties along the way and the loss of history in a church. Instead, come alongside a young worship leader to help him or her. That might give us a church that has the best of both worlds in worship. The "fight first, then capitulate" strategy is not God-honoring.

KEITH: I see what you are describing happening in some churches. I do think we could work together more to make the most of our worship opportunities.

DAVID: It is amazing for me to see the power of simply volunteering time in worship. If someone from the older generations cares about worship and doesn't want to see the grand traditions lost, the best strategy is to volunteer time to help in that area. They can make a big difference if they bring their talents and opinions to bear on the direction things are going. Offering time shows the older generations are willing to invest, not content to just be sideline critics of the worship.

KEITH: That makes great sense. So, let's list some questions together here that younger and older folk could talk about together to find greater common ground on music in worship.

Questions for Discussion

1. What songs have the deepest meaning to you personally? Why?

2. If you were facing a slow death with cancer, what songs would come to your mind as fortifying to your faith during a time of difficulty?

3. What songs from the past or present feel shallow to you? Why?

4. What is missing in the music at your worship service that you wish could be added?

5. What positive or negative symbolism does bright or dim lighting in worship communicate to you personally?

6. What do you think of worship venues where the musical style is targeted to one style preference?

7. What are the advantages and disadvantages to blended worship in a single worship service?

8. How can worship leaders of any age get feedback from the worshipers so they are helping all to worship the best they can?

9. What are the wrong and right things to do when worship music does not satisfy us?

10. How can people of all ages learn to be more pliable and accepting of the various languages of worship music?

11. Are there any older hymns that you wish younger people would learn the lyrics to?

12. Are there any new songs that you wish older people would learn the lyrics to?

2

Conversion

Why don't we have altar calls like we used to?

Is going to the altar too showy for people today?

We're supposed to report our conversion numbers annually. How can you count something like that?

Why haven't we seen people getting "gloriously saved" like we used to?

Why don't we have testimonies by new Christians anymore?

I'm worried about some of these new-style "authentic" testimonies younger folk give. Are they confessing too much publicly?

Is it wrong to use manipulative techniques to get people converted?

Have we made "becoming a Christian" too easy?

Are people claiming they're Christians without ever changing?

Can you really become a Christian simply by "making a decision"? Or is there more to it than that?

DAVID: While flipping channels for cartoons to watch with my kids one day we came across the Crystal Cathedral show. Filling my screen was the younger Schuller minister—not the white-haired one.

KEITH: Speaking of the generations needing to dialogue, didn't the older Schuller fire the younger one? Maybe there's a lesson in there for you. Don't offend your dad too much while he's still alive and kicking!

DAVID: Funny. Of course, even the younger Schuller seems a bit old to me—it's the grandson Schuller that's in the emerging generation. Anyway, let me tell my story. He posed in the sanctuary for the wide-camera shot as he held up a pocket-sized card from his wallet with the title "My Ticket to Heaven" on it. Schuller explained that wherever he goes he always carries this card with him. The camera zoomed in to show a line where he had signed his name. At that moment, the screen flashed an 800 number and instructions for how I could get a similar card for myself. I could call right then, get my ticket to heaven, and sign my name on it. It was that easy to sign up for salvation.

KEITH: Yes, I've seen this kind of thing.

DAVID: Man, this ticket-to-heaven approach to conversion makes us gag! I don't buy the quick and easy approach to salvation and most of my generation doesn't buy it either. Who invented this salvation microwave? Many of my peers just don't see why someone should "come down the aisle and decide it once and forever." We smirk because we all know those who went to dozens of altars to settle it forever. Many of us see following Jesus as a journey more than a decision.

KEITH: The ticket-to-heaven approach to evangelism is not really the holiness movement's traditional approach; we adopted it in the 1970s when it was the hot new thing (like the emerging innovations touted today). Back then, Billy Graham was having great rallies around the world. His radio program was titled "The Hour of Decision." Conversion gradually became more about making a decision than adopting a lifestyle. It was easy evangelism—just pray and you're in. About this time Bill Bright's *The Four Spiritual Laws* swept across the church. We were trained to do personal evangelism in order to "win the lost." The better-educated churches used D. James Kennedy's *Evangelism Explosion,* attractively packaged in a soft padded green book. Both methods went for a decision to accept Christ. These new methods of evangelism gave the impression that all it took was "praying the prayer." Campus Crusade sponsored Explo '72 (dubbed the "Christian Woodstock") in the Cotton Bowl where one hundred thousand young folk (I was in my late twenties) learned this new decision method of evangelism. The National Association of Evangelicals got on board by recruiting an emerging new group called "evangelicals" into KEY '73, a cooperative interdenominational evangelistic campaign to help people make a "decision to accept Christ." Most holiness churches got on board this new movement.

DAVID: OK, our generation is unaware of what happened before the 1970s. All we've known is this quick decision approach to evangelism. Many of us assume the ticket-to-heaven approach is all you ever had.

KEITH: Let me finish my story. It illustrates how churches adopt new approaches. In 1976, Bright launched *Here's Life America,* mobilizing church laity to present the gospel to every breathing person in North America, all supported by expensive billboards and slick newspaper advertising. By the end of the 1970s, these new methods of evangelism had completely swept across most holiness churches, displacing the traditional revival and altar-call approaches of the past. Evangelism was easy: go through a little booklet, lead the person in a short prayer, and "leave the results to God" as Bill Bright famously put it. Into this late '70s milieu came a bright young pastor from Ohio, John Maxwell. His GRADE program (Growth Resulting After Discipleship and Evangelism) and EPA seminars (Evangelism

Principles in Action) further reinforced the decision method. Wesleyan denominational leaders toted Maxwell around to every district, challenging people to go door to door with this new method of soul-winning. After someone made a decision, we were supposed to get the new convert to come on Sunday and walk the aisle—not in repentance, but as a public testimony to their already-made decision. Some churches even stapled basketball nets on the back wall after each new convert to keep score. Others lit a candle every Sunday there was a decision through the week.

DAVID: Now I know the actual meaning behind all those acronym conferences you talk about: KEY '73, GRADE, and EPA!

KEITH: Sure, feel free to mock us, but remember I could cite all the wacky names of your emerging church conferences that you think are so cool today.

DAVID: You've got me there. Thirty years later your acronym names sound dorky, but we mock our names after only three years! By the way, I remember several of the practices you talked about, including the salvation candle and the basketball nets. Actually, I must have experienced them ten years after they were introduced; by the time I saw them, they were the new traditions of the church.

KEITH: It works that way. Just wait until your emerging church plants start having twenty-five-year anniversaries, you'll start to feel old yourself. These new methods continued into the 1980s, with youth conventions like PACE '86 (People Answering the Call to Evangelism) challenging young people to "share your faith once a week until summer." In the 1970s and '80s, the ticket-to-heaven approach to evangelism was the hot new thing. It was a steamroller movement that flattened anyone who got in the way. Wesleyans, along with most others in the holiness movement, adopted this approach to evangelism. However, as I said above, it was not our traditional approach.

DAVID: Well, it may have been new, but this is the only kind of evangelism my generation ever experienced. To us it seems intellectually dishonest to think we can convert all kinds of different people using the same memorized rubric and four proof-texts nested in a nifty acronym. It oversimplifies what should be a spiritual—even mystical—transition of the soul. Calling someone down to an altar to get a heaven ticket seems ineffective to us. Door-to-door knocking, random witnessing, aggressive tracts, telemarketing campaigns, and competitive apologetics are tactics that seem downright offensive to lots of younger people. We think these methods might turn more people off than on. Obnoxious evangelism fits better with bizarre cults than the way of Jesus Christ. Maybe conversions chalked up this way are easier to count and celebrate, but many of us see no reason to keep this approach to evangelism. Conversion is more than making a quick decision—it is a journey to Christ.

KEITH: My only response on that point is that those methods are relatively new inventions in our churches.

DAVID: Then how did churches do evangelism before this?

KEITH: Before that, we used revivalist methods. Our churches expected a rigorous lifestyle from new converts and everyone knew it. Becoming a Christian meant resigning from lodges and giving up cigarettes, alcohol, and gambling. It meant starting to tithe and attending church three or four times a week, along with making a host of other lifestyle changes. The standard for entry was high. The unsaved knew what was expected of them before they were converted. They knew what they were going to get before they got saved.

When an altar call was given (often in a revival meeting) a person who was under conviction went to the altar, often with tears of repentance. Other Christians gathered around to help them "pray through." They stood up publicly to give a testimony of confession and commitment to live the life. Immediately they started attending church every time the doors opened and intended to become serious disciples. Back then, lives changed in a sudden transformation and continued to change even more over time. Becoming a Christian was more about entering a lifestyle than getting a ticket to heaven.

DAVID: When you remove some of the specific tactics and legalism and you just look at the results, that approach sounds a bit closer to what we desire now. We want real-life transformation, not just a simple decision with little expectation of change.

Another reason the microwave approach to conversion bothers us is that it does not seem to actually convert people. I have seen plenty of people walk the aisle or raise their hand to make a decision to accept Christ. I've gone to big conventions and rallies where hundreds swarm forward to "pray the prayer." However, we often see little difference in daily life of those who got their ticket to heaven. Conversion should change lives. It's more than a decision. It is a journey and a lifestyle.

KEITH: You're probably right. I suspect we thought the more people who prayed the prayer, the more might actually stick with it. Even though we adopted this method of evangelism, we still were generally more concerned with a holy lifestyle then a simple decision.

DAVID: Do you remember, Dad, when I was just thirteen years old and I went to one of the big youth conventions you mentioned—PACE? At that conference, my best friend and I committed to come home and witness every week. Our first week was passing by quickly and the guilt was mounting due to our unfulfilled promise. Finally, at lunch on Friday just hours from our deadline, we cornered one of our classmates (someone we had never much talked to before) and persuaded him read our tract and pray the prayer. Presto! We had our convert and kept our witnessing promise. I don't think we ever talked to him again about his commitment but we counted him. Maybe today he's a pastor, or maybe he's a prisoner. I have no idea. I still feel guilty about abandoning him, but on that day, we followed the directions and got a mark in the win column by coaxing him to get his ticket punched. That's the trouble with evangelism in the church: it is too much about a decision and not enough about relationships and life change.

KEITH: I think I see where you're going with this.

DAVID: I have not rejected the conversion microwave approach because I haven't tried it; I reject it because I *have* tried it and found it wanting. We've heard, "We have nothing to do but save souls." Your generation tried to teach us how win a soul, but your generation did not teach us how to make disciples.

KEITH: Yes, but I'll remind you that what you are wanting is square in the center of the historic approach of the holiness movement. We always expected real change in people until more recently when we adopted the decision approach. When it comes to your emphasis on the journey, I suppose the journey of earlier days took place mostly before a person was converted. There was often a long period of being under conviction before a person "broke" and repented. When they repented, they understood what kind of life they were expected to enter. It is very Wesleyan to expect real change in conversion.

DAVID: It's ironic. Perhaps if you had kept the revivalist approach you wouldn't have lowered the bar for conversion or adopted such a simplistic formula. That might have posed other problems (for instance, many of us still don't fully "get" the altar call thing), but it is interesting to speculate.

KEITH: Well, we abandoned revivalist methods for some good reasons. Many boomers thought the bar was too high. Back then, it seemed like a person had to become perfect before they could even become a Christian. We wanted to make it easier to get in the door, and then we intended to lead people further. The guilt motivation was what we wanted to get past. So we wanted to just get people in the door more quickly.

DAVID: I see the reasoning, but many never went further. They happily pocketed their heaven ticket and never changed. That kind of evangelism only vaccinates people against the real thing. They think they're saved because they prayed a prayer, yet they were never converted. You said the "unsaved knew what was expected" of them in the revivalist days. We resonate with that approach, even if we don't relate to all the methods. The problem with the present approach is its bait and switch tactic. In order to attract as many as possible, the bar is set so low that life-change is barely mentioned. Then that newcomer reads the Gospels and discovers the true cost of discipleship. There's a lot of fine print to your free gift. Many just cling to their ticket and forget fully following Christ. I understand your fear of legalism; I feel that too. But this more recent tactic is a bait and switch approach and many in my generation think it is deceitful.

KEITH: I agree that it is a problem. When we say, "All you've got to do is receive," we really have some small print in the backs of our minds. We actually think they should change too. Some go on, many don't; they get their ticket and plop down just inside the door—or, as you imply, maybe not even inside the door at all. We once expected regular testimonies from these people reporting on their victories. It was a sort of group accountability in prayer meetings.

DAVID: We love testimonies, and you should have never dumped them. Dad, I wonder if you guys abandoned testimonies because of your obsessive compulsion over excellence in worship services. You wanted the ordained ministers and musicians to run everything and couldn't stand ordinary people having stage time. If so, you exchanged real stories of truly changed lives for a fabricated and seamless standard of performance worship. I promise you this: My generation will bring back some form of testimony to highlight the unique journey of each follower of Christ. You can count on it. We may develop a radically different format from the one you grew up with, but there will be a shout out to fellow followers about their personal spiritual journey.

Just this evening I attended a late night Worship-and-Word gathering where a college student confessed to the whole room that he struggled with pornography and self-image issues, some stemming from his anger at his mother for abandoning him at birth. I was stunned to hear him share this in front of one hundred fifty of his peers. This was not a spur of the moment thing. It was a planned slot in the gathering. Testimonies are back. We have a testimony-shaped hole in our hearts.

KEITH: It will be interesting for us to watch. We saw plenty of abuses of the testimony time, so we sidelined it to prayer meeting. After the prayer meeting dribbled down, it mostly disappeared.

DAVID: Since the recent model was adopted before I was born, I don't think most of my generation ever witnessed the earlier model. The history I know is the one I have lived—your church, the one you gave me. We just don't get the ticket-punching, low-bar method of evangelism. My generation might adopt a completely new model. It sounds like yours did.

As we rediscover an authentic approach to evangelism, my generation will have its problems, just as your generation did. But you guys can help us, I hope. Your changes demonstrate that tradition can be altered.

KEITH: Exactly. Soon you will be making changes to the Church; then your kids will rise up to ask similar questions. Be wary—with every change, there come unintended consequences. Yet things still need to change, even if you are changing some things back to what my generation got rid of.

DAVID: Yes, our journey approach to conversion must be "edit-able." Perhaps we need to make sure our conversion model is fluid. For instance, it would be a mistake for us to be so taken up with the journey model that we make no room for overnight transformation. We'd then just trade microwave conversions for a crock-pot model that never boils. When someone shares that God freed him or her from an addiction in a moment, who are we to question that instant change? We also need to stay open to the past, not just be open to the future. We should be wary of creating another steamroller that flattens out all the old models with no respect for the wisdom they offer.

Perhaps the shared core value across both generations is true life-change. I suspect that life-change for your generation, Dad, emphasized the outer change (church involvement, quitting bad habits, etc.). Younger generations hold the same core life-change value in conversion, but we'll emphasize inner change as primary, along with relational changes. Nevertheless, I think we both might agree that in the end, conversion is all about change. At least it should be.

KEITH: Yes, *that* we have in common. Conversion changes things—not just on the books in heaven, but in real lives here and now.

History can be changed. We know this! Our generation radically changed the Church from what we inherited. Your generation will change it too. Our innovations quickly became traditions. The church you were raised in is not the church in which we were raised. We saw things that needed to be changed, and we changed them (sometimes for the better, sometimes for the worse). Now your generation sees changes that need to be made to our changes. That's fair.

Just remember, your innovations will quickly become tomorrow's traditions, the traditions your children will rise up to critique. If you can find a better balance, your own kids will have less to change. Both of our generations want real life change. We lowered the bar for entry, maybe too low. Your generation is now raising the bar with a journey spin, and emphasizing the severity of relational sin. I'm glad you want to stay fluid. After all, you guys don't have the final solution either.

DAVID: Yes, we need to stay fluid. As a representative of the older generations, what advice do you have as we try to reintroduce some sort of public testimony?

KEITH: My generation would warn of some bad effects with confessional testimonies (as opposed to victory testimonies). Your hunger for authenticity in telling everything publicly can simply make all the other sinners feel more comfortable in their sin. "Everybody seems to have this problem—it must be normal." But average Christianity is not normal Christianity. Confessional testimonies can create an atmosphere where sinners compete to give the gooiest story like some sort of Sinner's American Idol. Confessing sin gives less glory to God than testifying about God's deliverance from sin.

DAVID: Yes, my generation needs to learn that lesson: Authenticity should be empowered by victory. I suppose people sharing their current sin is not any more authentic than people sharing their current victory over a sin they've "put to death." We should highlight stories by Christians who tell about winning over sin. Those foster faith in God's deliverance. Authentic community should promote spiritual maturity. Testimonies may be making a comeback, but older generations who fear abuse must restrain their suspicion. We younger generations must be wary of the kind of authenticity that results in sin-glorification, but the goal is for more testimonies of deliverance. I suppose the hunger for authenticity can lower the bar on sin just as the older generations lowered the bar on conversion with the ticket-to-heaven approach.

KEITH: Exactly. If you keep that in mind, you'll keep the pendulum from swinging back into another excess on the other side.

DAVID: But what about the way we talk about salvation being a journey. I have sensed many in the older generations are uncomfortable with that kind of talk.

KEITH: Well, we hope you do not abandon the possibility of a momentary dramatic life change because of your bias toward the gradual change of the journey approach. All process and no instantaneous is no better than all instantaneous and no process. People really can be delivered from pornography, eating disorders, or alcohol in a moment. It may not happen each time with each person that way, but it can happen. If you can't find any younger people with such a testimony, invite some older folk to come to your gatherings to tell their story. Such a guest testimony might increase the faith of the younger crowd for dramatic deliverance. Even if you reject this shorter way of life-change, at least allow our generation to claim it. Don't scoff at us as if we've made it up.

We hope you won't box God in with your own preference for a gradual journey. Allow for God to work both ways: gradually and in a single moment. We worry that the gradual approach to conversion may never get people across the line at all. Our most recent read-the-prayer approach had weaknesses, we admit, but it did have a line to cross. We hope your generation can baptize a person who is now in the family, not just a person headed that way. There is a line to be crossed, even if one heads toward the line for a while and keeps journeying after crossing that line. You may approach conversion with a longer period of gestation, but eventually we hope the baby gets born!

DAVID: Yes, my generation's leaders must find a way for people to cross the line; we agree on that. All generations should be wary of the empty signs of conversion like reading a prayer or going forward or raising a hand if there is no life change. And we also must worry about conversion journeys that never pass any milestones of assurance. In the rush to reject easy-conversions, we could forget there is any line at all to cross. I admit my generation is guilty of this. There is a moment when new life begins even if it is after a long season of development. It may not have to be walking the aisle, but conversion still needs to involve a public confirmation of change.

KEITH: Amen! I don't know if we're closer to being on the same page yet in this discussion or not. At least we hit on some common values and some deeper questions to ask. I think we can both agree that there are few things as crucial as why, how, and when a person is converted. I hope you younger folk can find a balance as you take over the Church. Let's list some questions here to start the ongoing conversation in a local church between the generations.

Questions for Discussion

1. What are the strengths of the ticket-to-heaven or decision approach to evangelism? What are the weaknesses?

2. What were the strengths of the revival altar call approach to evangelism? Weaknesses?

3. What are the strengths of the journey approach to evangelism? Weaknesses?

4. Search for and make a list of the ways people were converted in Scripture. What similarities are there? What differences?

5. What do you think of churches numerically reporting conversions at the end of a church year? How do we know a person is converted?

6. Are more people getting saved gradually today than in the past? How does a person get saved gradually? What kind of cross-the-line moments should a church offer for people?

7. The oldest folk in a church and the younger ones often like personal testimonies or narrative approaches. Why do many in between not like this approach? What are the dangers of authentic testimonies?

8. What are some ideas for the future for helping people become truly converted and not just getting their ticket punched?

9. Considering evangelism in our own church, what should be left as it is? What should we change?

10. How can the church do better at making disciples, not just making converts?

3

Community

Why can't I get connected at this church?

Why are we shutting down the Sunday night and Wednesday night services?

How come young folk say they yearn for community, yet they skip Sunday school?

Why don't the older folk mentor me?

I'm confused; the young folk say they want to be connected, but they don't show up for anything we offer.

What happened to a good old-fashioned potluck? I used to love those—such a good way to get connected.

I have been coming here for two years, and if I stopped coming next week, I bet no one would notice for six months.

Don't these young folk know we have other things to do beside hang out at the church—we're busy!

In the smaller church where I was raised, I knew everyone; now that we have multiple services I never see the young couples.

DAVID: Most in my generation think the church should be more of a community than it is. We think of the church as a people who "do life together" and not just an event we attend. The church should be like a family that loves, shares, works, and plays together. Most of the churches we grew up in were event-focused churches, offering programs to attend and watch more than living as a true Christian community.

KEITH: I see what you are saying. My generation had a great deal of such "community" when we were growing up. In fact, many of us had no life outside the church. We attended Sunday school, Sunday morning worship, Sunday evening service, Wednesday night prayer meeting, and we showed up at two week-long revival meetings a year and a "watch night" service every New Year's Eve in the sanctuary where we waited for the new year in prayer. We went to each other's homes after Sunday evening service for snacks and fellowship. In addition, our churches had fellowship halls where just about any special occasion from Mother's Day to Valentine's Day was an excuse to eat and share together. Many in my generation actually felt the church was too ingrown in its community. So, as we adopted the busy life, we dropped many of these routines. That made more time for connecting with the world and for outreach and evangelism.

DAVID: That is fascinating. You had something that we crave. I can see how it could become ingrown, however. That's a constant struggle for going deeper in community. Unfortunately, it seems like the pendulum has swung far over to the other side. In too many churches the gathering is more like a performance or movie that people attend and watch rather than a place where you connect with your best friends and experience *koinonia*.

KEITH: Well, by the time we cancelled many of these community activities, we had already made our friends. We continued fellowship with the friends we'd already made in the church.

DAVID: That's the problem. There's plenty of room for fellowship among those who already have friends at church, but making friends is still difficult for new people and for younger people. My generation has a deep yearning for intimacy and community. We want to be a part of a larger family who knows each other and cares about even the smallest details. I'll be honest, breaking into friendship at boomer churches is hard.

KEITH: Well, your generation could start by attending Sunday evening service or prayer meetings where they still exist.

DAVID: Ouch—you got me there. We're pretty absent at those. But I'll admit we see these programs as mostly designed for older people. They just sit and listen to someone talk. These meetings aren't as much about creating community as listening to one more sermon or one more lesson. How do you develop community lined up in rows listening to someone talk at you?

KEITH: Sure, many of these services are aimed at the people who attend them. However, if younger folk attended, maybe the content and style might shift to meet the needs of the younger generation?

DAVID: Maybe, but I doubt it. Have you ever tried to change the format of one of those services? Good luck!

We are generally dissatisfied with just going to church services. The philosophy of most services seems to be "come and sit and listen." We hunger for the kind of authentic *koinonia* that develops on a mission trip. When we've returned from something like that, we try to find it in the church, but everyone checks in, watches the service, then goes home to their own life and friends.

KEITH: It didn't used to be that way. The services many of us grew up on were highly relational. We grew up going to prayer meetings where the preacher never even preached, and the entire group gave testimonies updating the church on what was happening in their life. When I was a kid, almost every person attending a prayer meeting was expected to give a testimony. Then we had prayer requests, and we heard about people and their spiritual needs. Sometimes they told about the spiritual needs of people who weren't even there. Then we had a season of prayer where almost everyone, one after another, prayed aloud. People even prayed for "backsliders" by name in these prayer meetings. When we left, we knew a lot (sometimes more than we wanted to know) about all the others attending and those who had skipped.

DAVID: Never in my life have I seen that in church. If prayer meetings were like that today, I think many young people would show up. It sounds exactly like what we do in our small groups. Why did you get rid of this approach?

KEITH: Because of the abuses we saw. We thought people talked too much about themselves and attracted too much attention. Sometimes they said embarrassing things in their testimonies. The prayers were sometimes repetitive and vacant of meaning. An increasing number of people were busy and didn't want to invest an hour to hear someone who hadn't prepared. We gradually moved to a Bible study led by the professional pastor and reduced participation from the people.

DAVID: So where do people share these sorts of things in today's church? If it isn't happening somewhere, don't people miss out on becoming a tight group? Much of the model for deep friendships in my generation comes from TV and the movies. When we think of "doing life together," we don't think of church as much as the shows we watched when we were growing up (depending on our age) like *Cheers*, *Seinfeld*, or *Friends*. The coming-of-age movies for a whole generation were stories of friendship and community in unlikely places, like *The Breakfast Club* or *St. Elmo's Fire*. Later on, kids are coming of age weaned on their own experiences of friendship and community in a confusing world with shows like *Lost* and *Friday Night Lights*. Shouldn't the body of Christ offer friendship and community that is more powerful than these films and TV shows that are little more than passing fads?

KEITH: It should and much more. Perhaps we have failed to see the need for deeper intimacy in the younger generation, especially now that so many are delaying marriage to their late twenties and even early thirties. Most of my generation got married in the first half of our twenties. Now that marriage is being delayed, maybe more has to be done for singles.

DAVID: Certainly for singles, but also for young married people. All younger adults hunger for this kind of community and many think the church has failed them. Some of the loneliest and most troubled people are newlyweds. They find more community at their workplace or among their school friends than at church.

KEITH: So why doesn't your generation start something? Most churches would be delighted if young folk started a small group, or a MOPS group, or if five young adults started a breakfast club. It seems to my generation that the younger ones expect aging boomers to start everything for them, as if we're still their parents providing activities for children.

DAVID: OK, that's a fair criticism—and fairly accurate. It is true that many of us expect the church to provide things for us. We are slow to take the initiative and start them ourselves. We think you expect us to fit into the program you already have going, especially at larger churches that seem to be offering something for everyone except us.

KEITH: It's true that my generation might expect you to fit into our programming. We sometimes say, "Why don't they show up?" Yet many of us are quite willing for your generation to start *new* programs. If you want to meet on Sunday night and do something different, many churches would be delighted. If you want to start something on what used to be prayer meeting night, why not start it? What kind of things ought to happen to provide the friendship and ongoing intimacy that you guys hunger for?

DAVID: Some churches commission a younger pastor on staff to start a new service that focuses more on participation and community (you'd be surprised at how many testimonies you'd hear there!). Other churches are doing meals together—meals that are intergenerational, that help us connect. It might make sense for churches to use small groups or more intentional Sunday school classes to help people to connect.

KEITH: Many churches would be happy to see those kinds of things happen. If young adults in their twenties and thirties just started them, I think most my age would be quite happy. Few churches say no when someone wants to start a new Sunday school class.

DAVID: But we aren't just starving for relationships with other young adults, we want full-orbed relationships, with older folk too.

KEITH: Then invite some of those older folk attending the Sunday night service to whatever you start. Some would come. Many of them would love to develop friendships with young adults. The reason many of us boomers don't intrude is we think your generation is like ours was. When we were young, many of us just wanted to be left alone. Hey, my generation invented youth ministry—splitting off the teens for a separate meeting and programs. Many of the boomer pastors today started out as youth ministers, and all we wanted from the rest of the church was to be left alone to do our thing. When we leave young adults alone, we think we're doing you a favor.

DAVID: Well, we don't want you controlling what we do, I suppose, but we like relating to older folk too and feel something is missing when we only hang out with people our age. That feels kind of shallow and counterfeit. My generation complains that older adults don't take time to mentor us and help us along.

KEITH: Mentoring is a good example. Many boomers weren't mentored by the generation before them. We simply took over and mentored each other along the way; boomers mentoring boomers. Perhaps we need help in becoming mentors to the younger adults. How should we do this?

DAVID: Well, I think your general admonition that we need to take some responsibility is key here. I remember once when I complained to my accountability partner that my senior pastor wasn't mentoring me, he asked, "Well, do you have a meeting with him for that?" I was confused. I expected the mentoring to be more of a "life on life" thing, like an impromptu "Hey, want to go grab some coffee and chat" kind of mentoring. My friend said, "Well, if you don't have a meeting scheduled, you'll never get a boomer to mentor you." From that point on, I've always tried to schedule that stuff, and I've never found a boomer who wasn't willing to carve out some time.

KEITH: That's an important observation. Yes, we boomers are often slaves to our calendars, so getting on the calendar makes it a priority.

DAVID: I suspect younger people have never learned what I heard from my friend. So they are twisting in the wind and wondering why those they wish would mentor them don't seem to care. I wonder if you boomers could go halfway and offer to have a mentoring meeting— to get the conversation started.

KEITH: I think there are boomers who do that, though many of us might think inviting you to be mentored is acting superior to you in some way.

Mentoring the next generation is an important task at our stage of life. However, understand this: Many boomers still pretend we are young. Just like your own generation has delayed moving into full adulthood by a decade, we have delayed moving into senior adulthood by a decade, or maybe even more. Many boomers feel like they just took over, and we are still trying to establish our revolution. Boomers still leading 1980s style worship call it "contemporary," even though the style is twenty or more years old. We probably need to wake up and see retirement coming at us faster than a speeding locomotive.

DAVID: While in seminary, my wife and I attended about fifteen churches in the Boston area trying to find a Christian community to call home. The one we finally landed at wasn't any better than the others, and in many ways was worse. The difference? The pastor invited us with about five other young people and a few established families to his house after the service. Wow! That was impressive. We chose to attend that church even though the preaching was average, the facility was decrepit, the music was out-of-touch, the pews were uncomfortable, we didn't know a soul attending there, and—on top of all this—I was a Wesleyan preparing for the ministry and it was an American Baptist Church! But that relational invitation made the difference for us. The leaders of a church (whether it's the pastor or the lay people) can have a lot of influence by just making short intentional connections with younger generations this way.

KEITH: Great story! However, in larger churches there are too many for the pastor to connect with by him- or herself. So initiating the connection yourself is still important instead of waiting for an invitation. More young adults might consider inviting the pastor to *their* house for a cookout!

Help me out here. What are some of the things that we should start together to develop greater *koinonia*?

DAVID: Beyond worship, small groups, and classes, the two best ways are eating together and working together. Nothing binds people together quite like a meal. We've all made fun of the church potluck for so long we've forgotten the whole point was to create a space where conversations between families and generations can take place. Common meals, love feasts, weekly suppers, and after-church potlucks may need to make a big comeback. Second, doing community-service-type-projects or going on intergenerational mission trips would help address my generation's hunger for community.

KEITH: Those are good ideas and some churches are doing that. Maybe your generation can inspire us to do more. Why not prod us by volunteering to lead it? If young adults want a common meal at church every week they shouldn't expect the boomers to do all the work preparing, serving, and cleaning up. Your generation needs to pitch in too, or maybe even lead the whole thing yourselves and then invite the boomers.

DAVID: So part of what I'm hearing is that in our quest for greater community in the church, we must avoid becoming ingrown. If we can connect through service and outreach, that will help. You are also saying my generation needs to start some of this on our own. We need to be willing to step up and lead this change. Your generation will probably help by giving some of your leadership horsepower as well as your blessing. From the way you described the generations older than you, maybe they'll see this happening and will simply say, "Well, it's about time you got back to doing church the right way."

KEITH: Yep, that's the way I see it. We're pretty far into this discussion but there are probably other things to discuss. Let's list some questions that younger and older folk could talk about together on this subject to bring us closer together.

Questions for Discussion

1. Describe the kind of community you experienced in the church where you were raised. If you grew up unchurched, where did you find community?

2. Tell about the most significant community you experienced in this church in the last few years. What made this experience stand out for you?

3. If a people started attending this church on Sunday mornings and wanted to break into friendship, what would he or she need to do beyond attending a service? How would he or she know this?

4. About what size group is ideal for developing close community? How big does a group have to get before it is too large for creating intimate friendships?

5. What role does family play in community? If people have lots of relatives nearby, how does it help or hinder making new friendships?

6. What groups does our church already have that provide community for those in them?

7. About how many people do you think you can have a deep friendship with?

8. Who are your deepest friends in life now—those you share most openly with? How many are in this church?

9. What might we do in our church's regularly scheduled services and programming to promote the development of greater *koinonia*?

10. In what sort of setting here at our church do people over age sixty-five experience community? Singles under thirty? Those with small children? Those who are middle-aged or empty nesters?

11. What new groups could be formed in our church to provide greater friendships and intimacy among our people? Who might be the likely person to start them?

12. In what way has this group—the group studying this book—become friends and developed deeper connection?

4

Race

Why is Sunday morning worship the most segregated hour in the week?
Why do our promotional pictures look more diverse than we really are?
I'm tired of all this diversity talk; it's just being politically correct.
Why don't we have more African-Americans in leadership?
Why are we making such a big deal about racial issues?
Should our committees have quotas now?
Isn't there a latent racism that lies as an undercurrent in our churches?
True integration is never going to happen; why beat our heads against a wall?
Our denomination fought for the abolition of slavery—shouldn't that count?

DAVID: One thing I've noticed is that the younger generations seem to care deeply about the sin of racism that is an undercurrent in many churches, but older generations seem more casual about it.

KEITH: Hey, our denomination was at the forefront of the abolition movement. That is the major reason Wesleyan Methodists became a denomination in 1843.

DAVID: I'm not talking about 1843; I'm talking about now.

When I was on a district board of ministerial development, we once interviewed a guy for his ordination. This man had entered the ministry from an engineering career, picked up his life and headed off to Asbury Seminary. His answers to the form questions were excellent, and he had a solid reputation as an effective preacher. He was a slam dunk for ordination. He also was black. So we had the obligatory race discussion. We asked questions such as, "How has your race affected your ministry" and "How has your race been a factor in the denomination?" He spoke admiringly about the history related to abolition of slavery in The Wesleyan Church. After the ice was broken, we asked, "How do you think you can help us regain our role in race issues, since we are overwhelmingly white as a denomination?"

KEITH: OK, I know the guy you're talking about. He preached at our church last year. He was a really good preacher.

DAVID: Yes, that's him. Well, this pastoral candidate paused for a long moment with a thoughtful smile on his face then said something like this:

> Yes, the history of abolition of slavery is there, and I've heard a lot about that. However, something that I think many black people out there think about is the absence of The Wesleyan Church in the civil rights movement. It seems like we have to go back pretty far in history to find Wesleyans that cared about the issues African-Americans were facing. Maybe the place for us to start is by confessing our lack of involvement in those key days—instead of always going back to abolition as though everything was solved then. Perhaps we need to start by saying we're sorry for not showing up when it counted.

Our board sat in stunned silence as we recognized the truth of his words. So why is this true? You were around in the 1960s. Why was The Wesleyan Church present in 1843, when abolition of slavery was the cause, and yet so silent when it had to do with extending voting rights, opening up fair housing for blacks, banning segregation in schools, and allowing human rights for blacks like using the same drinking fountains and sitting in the same bus seats as white people?

KEITH: Your pastor-friend is right. Wesleyans were largely AWOL in the fight for civil rights in the 1960s. He is also right that we never have fully confessed that. In the 1960s, Wesleyans were highly susceptible to political calls for law and order. There were radicals and hippies marching against the Vietnam War and gathering at Woodstock in upstate New York, where they took off their clothes and smoked pot and celebrated free love. Yet at the same time, there were marches for civil rights.

Wesleyans were just gaining a newfound respectability and many saw marching as radical agitating, and they were told that all this was inspired by communists. Many Wesleyans joined other evangelicals in becoming law-and-order Christians. They disengaged from any activism at all. Most did not oppose the Vietnam War or push for civil rights, which were seen as similar causes. Wesleyans in the 1960s were just as susceptible to political influence as they are today. Just look at recent political campaigns to see how susceptible Wesleyans are to political leaders. Back then, the civil rights movement was seen like today's movement to extend rights to illegal immigrants. Wesleyans took their signals more from political leaders than from their own heritage, the Bible, or even from their own leaders. Unfortunately we were largely absent, but not totally so.

DAVID: If not totally absent, then who are we talking about? I hear stories of Wesleyan heroes of abolition. Where are the stories of those who fought for civil rights for African-Americans?

KEITH: Wesleyans like Bob Black and Jo Anne Lyon weren't absent. Neither was I. Not all Wesleyans were AWOL during the civil rights movement. I took my turn marching and participated in what were then called "demonstrations" during the '60s. Some of us were considered dangerous by the law-and-order Wesleyans, yet we escaped retribution. Why? Because we were quietly protected by denominational leaders who remembered our heritage. These leaders may not have marched themselves, but they did provide protection for those who did. However, I admit there were not many. It is something we ought to confess. We mostly stood by silently.

DAVID: If that is the case, is it honest to proudly proclaim our one-hundred-fifty-year-old abolition history when we did not show up when blacks needed us more recently?

KEITH: Perhaps we do so because we feel guilty for not showing up more recently. I agree we may need to confess we were mostly a no-show during the more recent civil rights movement.

DAVID: Well, let me ask you about this: At one of our general conferences, Dr. Bob Black of Southern Wesleyan University (whom you just mentioned) gave a wonderful presentation including great stories about our abolitionist history. That presentation asked, "Who are we as Wesleyans?" then answered with "We are who we were." My generation thinks that slogan is more hopeful than truthful. In reality, we are nothing like what we were, right?

KEITH: Honestly, we are not. Wesleyans are a moving target. We change under the influence of movements in the broader church and even in the secular world. In 1843, we were unanimous in fighting the three hottest social issues of the day—the sin of slavery, the alcohol trade, and the right of women to be ordained. After the Civil War, other social issues swept across Christendom, including fighting against oath-bound secret societies. Wesleyans did not freeze in our founding issues. We moved with the rest of North American Christianity. We got caught up in anti-Masonry like most other Christians. Wesleyans did not freeze in that either. We were influenced by every new social issue that arose. We are right now caught up in the current social issues of opposing abortion and gay marriage. Wesleyans are not just who we were but we are who we are, and we are heavily influenced by Christian books, Christian radio, political leaders, and even secular talk shows. By 1963, 120 years had passed since the founding of our denomination. The Wesleyans of the 1960s weren't made up of the original abolitionists; they were mostly new converts and transfers from other denominations. We are who we are, and your friend is right in observing that we were not at the forefront of the 1960s civil rights movement. Perhaps we shouldn't tout our abolition history so much, though I wouldn't want to hide it either.

DAVID: Exactly. It seems to me that the moment race issues are mentioned, Wesleyans pull the ripcord on our abolitionist parachute and hope for a soft landing. Many in my generation think Wesleyans should (1) confess our mistakes and sins of omission and (2) make progress in actual diversity in our churches and leadership structures.

KEITH: Many of us in the older generations would agree. Maybe your generation will write the confession and lead the service some day. Maybe your generation will show us the way to greater racial diversity on our church staffs. At least give us credit for what we have written on paper; we have consistently and soundly condemned racism in our membership commitments as sin. So at least theoretically, we have made this a membership issue just like alcohol and other lifestyle issues.

DAVID: Yes, our theological and social positions are clear in written form. And Wesleyans got it right on abolition. I don't mean to belittle that admirable history—I'm sorry if I'm pressing too hard on this one. When it comes to this issue, perhaps we have simply not preached on the sin of racism enough. When sin is not condemned, we quietly let that sin slip by.

KEITH: Well, we don't preach directly about sin much at all, let alone racism. I'm not hearing your generation preach about sin much either.

DAVID: We certainly have not heard much about sin, except for the sins of teenagers; most preachers ignore the sins of those who tithe.

KEITH: In some ways I see your generation condemning sin even more than mine, you're just condemning different sins.

DAVID: Yes, we would condemn the sin of racism faster than worry about some of the other rules.

KEITH: So be it. Every generation picks and chooses what they see as the most dangerous current sins. Of course, all sin is dangerous. As your generation takes over the pulpits, you will have your chance to preach about whatever sin the Lord lays on your heart. Of course, you cannot pronounce yourselves heroes because all of culture is behind you on this one—racism is a popular sin to condemn.

DAVID: True, my generation may be swayed by cultural forces and political correctness just as past generations were when they opposed drinking a drop of alcohol or joining oath-bound lodges. Of course, just because something becomes politically correct doesn't mean it's automatically wrong. And many are discovering that this issue is often *not* politically correct in the real world of church boards, pastoral search committees, and district and denominational politics. In many churches, the suggestion to consider hiring a minority still causes a massive behind-closed-doors debate. My generation thinks at the core of this reaction is the sin of racism.

KEITH: You are right, that this is sin. The church is not completely free of board members who sin.

DAVID: Yes, when an individual espouses stuff like that, it's a sin; when entire boards function in this way, it's a sinful conspiracy. But, you see my point. Let's move on to solutions. Where do you think our two generations come together in the future? What can we agree on with this issue?

KEITH: We can agree that racism is sin and we have some racism still among us, among my generation and in your generation too.

DAVID: Agreed; my generation is better at pointing out the sins of older generations than seeing our own. But, can you agree that we have some unfinished confessing to do?

KEITH: By all means. Not only confession, maybe we owe some restitution too, which is a real sign of repentance. How about your generation? Can you join us in confession and restitution, or are you guys perfectly pure?

DAVID: We have some confessing to do too. Because opposing racism is so politically correct, some of my own generation have reacted against it and held on to a counter-political attitude toward other races, often times using code words that race-bait a conversation. We emerging generations have also made a lot of noise about race but haven't done much to build authentic relationships across racial lines. I wonder if every generation may feel their parents are more racist than they are. Maybe our children will roll their eyes at us as well.

KEITH: I assure you that your children will do plenty of eye rolling. But your own generation will very soon take over the church. What are your hopes for the future of the church concerning race?

DAVID: I would like to see an official worship service of confession and hope that would include some readings and realistic statements that summarize what we're saying here; people of color could help us publicly cast a vision for the future. We could also do some work in our local congregations to build bridges with churches that are predominantly made up of other races. We could also give a more prominent role to people of color and minorities in our representative leadership. This all sounds politically correct, but sometimes the politically correct thing is also biblically correct. Sometimes the culture really does catch up to the biblical trajectory of the kingdom of God. The goal is not to be politically correct; it's for the church to more accurately reflect heaven on earth.

KEITH: So how can my generation bless and support you as you lead us in that direction?

DAVID: Your generation can privately give us advice on doing all this for the right reasons. Help us seek true change to become more like the diverse kingdom of God. Those who were on the right side of history in civil rights could also step out of the shadows and tell their stories to us (in blogs or in Wesleyan periodicals); instead of confessing wrong with the rest of us they could admit they were right. I would love us to have someone to thank. So, how can our younger generation help the older generation in this journey?

KEITH: You can ask my generation to tell you our stories. You can judge yourselves along with judging us; we both have room for repentance and improvement on the matter of race. You can be a model to us in your youth, developing or planting diverse churches we can admire and support. You can elect one of your own minorities as a denominational leader and invite them to speak at your youth conventions. Don't let anyone look down on you for your youth, but be an example for all believers—even for the older generation. We can become what you envision.

DAVID: So, as people discuss this touchy chapter in their churches, what are some of the questions we should list to prompt honest discussion?

Questions for Discussion

1. Were you around during the civil rights years? What do you remember about the debates and the context back then? Did you speak up then?

2. What lingering problems related to race are there in your community?

3. What should the role of your church be when it comes to racial tensions in a community?

4. What is the largest racial minority in your community?

5. What could we do in the future as a denomination to ensure we are dealing with race in a way that honors God?

6. How would we know when we've gone too far in this discussion about race? Is there a risk of being too politically correct here?

7. Have you ever been to a racial reconciliation service? What was good and bad about that experience?

8. If you or your group were assigned the task to design a race confession service like the one discussed in this chapter, what elements would you include that would be meaningful? (Write this plan on a separate sheet of paper.)

9. What are the issues today that young adults are being silent on that our children might ask us if we were present or absent?

5

Heaven

I think our obsession with the rapture is just escapism—an ejection seat from responsibility for earth and its people.

Some time ago preachers stopped talking about hell; now they don't even talk about heaven.

I think more about heaven now that I'm older, but I wish I knew more about it. I seldom hear anything on the subject.

The whole idea of floating around on clouds and strumming harps is not for me. I seldom think about heaven.

Heaven was once the goal of life, then it became a reward for living right, and now it is hardly mentioned at all.

I believe in heaven, sure, but I think too much heaven-talk takes people's mind off what God expects them to do here and now.

KEITH: We boomers admire you younger generations for your practical approach to the here and now. After all, we boomers are a practical lot ourselves. However, some of us boomers (and more so, those older than boomers) wonder if you are forgetting the importance of heaven and the afterlife in your preaching and teaching. You sometimes treat these truths as if they are minor doctrines. Admittedly, older folk are closer to entering the afterlife than you, but heaven and the life beyond this life is not something dreamed up by our generation. It's a longstanding orthodox Christian doctrine since the early church.

DAVID: I hear what you're saying about doctrine, but much of the focus on heaven and hell isn't really doctrine; it's sensationalism. Sometimes it has been done to stoke fear in people to get them saved, to scare people about the penalty of hell, or to stir up desire for promising rewards. Heaven-talk has even been done with too much focus on the end times, as if the preacher has figured out all the prophecies in the book of Revelation. Maybe what you see as a de-emphasis on heaven is really just putting heaven in its proper theological place. We have to live in the here and now, instead of always thinking about the afterlife.

KEITH: Those excesses may be a problem, but losing focus on the afterlife gives the impression that religion is a human and temporal thing and that this present life is all that matters. That doesn't fit with classic orthodoxy. Jesus, Paul, and the early church fathers saw the afterlife as central to Christian teaching. Downplaying the afterlife might cater to young folk who can't imagine death and dying, but it robs older folk of the hope of "a heaven to gain and a hell to shun." Christianity is more than merely a better way to live on earth—it is a true promise of everlasting life beyond this life.

DAVID: OK, we do need to incorporate heaven theology in an intentional way in our teaching, but part of what's needed is a deconstruction of incorrect views. We'd rather talk about transforming our world today, about how we can bring the kingdom of heaven to earth. We pray that in the Lord's Prayer—"Thy kingdom come; thy will be done *on earth.*" My generation is all about the business of seeing God's will done on earth as it is in heaven, so we think we are balancing heaven and earth.

KEITH: But your approach can give the wrong impression that usefulness is what counts: doing something here and now. What about an old woman suffering with chronic pain who can't volunteer for any of the delightful new initiatives offered by her emergent pastor? Is she useless or does a person like her have worth as a person, and not just for what she does? We say we are pro-life and the fetus has dignity because it is a person; but will we extend this worth-in-being to the other end of life? An exclusive emphasis on the here-and-now enshrines works as the greatest value and not personhood. Ignoring heaven robs Christians from this larger and longer view.

DAVID: I think that's a good corrective. Perhaps we've just not experienced enough life yet to achieve this balance in teaching doctrine. So, theology is one thing. On the other hand, when there are whole sermons and emotional songs about heaven, it's over-emphasized; it can feel almost coercive. I suppose we're trying to say that heaven is part of the benefit of the Christian life, but it's not central. The afterlife should not be the motivation, positive or negative, for us today.

KEITH: I disagree. Preaching and teaching about heaven reminds us of the eternal. The eternal is central, not peripheral. This life on earth is not the whole. Heaven is the goal of life for the Christian, not a reward. Why ignore the whole and emphasize the part? Certainly it is true that we can be so heavenly minded that we are no earthly good, but we can also be so earthly minded that we make heaven irrelevant. Whatever is overlooked by the preachers eventually ceases to be believed by the laity. If we seldom speak of heaven, we will eventually come to funerals to celebrate the person's life. We will remember their good influence rather than speaking of heaven, eternity, and the resurrection. This is the kind of funerals atheists have, not Christians.

Atheists look back at their funerals; Christians look ahead. Atheists say, "She lives on in our memory." Christians say we can look forward to a coming resurrection and heaven. If we seldom hear of heaven, we will gradually quit believing there is such a thing and our funerals will be the first to show it.

DAVID: OK, maybe funerals are where the rubber meets the road in this discussion. In the same way that a Good Friday sermon reveals one's theology of the cross, a funeral sermon reveals one's theology of the afterlife. I haven't heard many compelling funeral sermons from my generation now that you mention it.

KEITH: It's good to hear you admit that. I hesitated bringing it up.

DAVID: No sense getting shy with your critique. Have at it, that's what this book is about.

KEITH: I think the biggest reason we need to hear more of heaven and eternity is to know that God is good. If we don't believe in eternity, we must eventually conclude that God is a devil. Really! How could a good God let injustice and pain prevail? The only way we can believe God is good is to hear of the afterlife when God will ultimately make all things right. Wrongs will be punished, right will be rewarded, but more importantly, the world will be restored. Sure, God is starting that here and now, and we must join him as you urge, but the work will not be finished until eternity. Forgetting to talk about heaven, judgment, and the resurrection will eventually make us doubt the goodness of God. Why couldn't the younger preachers give at least one full sermon a year on this important truth?

DAVID: Well, I've preached two sermons in the last three years on heaven—and I think you heard one of them. Perhaps it's a disagreement with the content I'm preaching—not the frequency.

The justice approach may be the key here. The younger generations may not have a keen sense of the afterlife, but we do have a keen sense of justice, and I agree with you that our theology of justice must include the righting of wrongs in eternity. However, the problem is when the older generation wants the end times to do all the justice work for them. We believe that God has enlisted us to do kingdom transformation work in the here and now. It seems like your generation just wants to let the world go to hell in a hand-basket and let the rapture clean up the mess. As long as you're heaven-bound, you don't seem to care about the rest.

KEITH: That is a fair critique. I admit that some of us simply stand by and watch the world deteriorate hoping to get beamed up to heaven and escape the mess. However, it is not true of us completely; we've worked like crazy to get people saved. We have been evangelistic not just because being a Christian is a better way to live (though it is), but also because of the promise of heaven.

DAVID: But doesn't a heaven-motivation run dry eventually? It's not enough to save a person *from* something; we've got to save them *for* something. So, our theology should include the afterlife, but we have to do something in this life to bring the kingdom into reality.

KEITH: Explain that more.

DAVID: What if all our focus on heaven really misses much of the point? When Christ talks about the end times or when Scripture points to heaven, it's always to motivate us to change things in the here and now. It is not just to convert people, but to bring about heaven on earth. Missing this part is why so many in our culture today think of heaven as such a boring afterlife. Scripture speaks of heaven descending to earth too, as a New Jerusalem. Heaven isn't just about escaping to somewhere else. This kind of kingdom of God is what many of us want to bring about.

KEITH: I do agree that the kingdom of God is seen in Scripture as both later and now. And I agree that perhaps we have too much forgotten the now aspects and emphasized only the later aspects. But you have to admit that there will be an end—the beginning of the afterlife, right?

DAVID: Well, younger generations are reevaluating end times stuff. We're wondering if the church has missed part of its responsibility to be a foreshadowing of heaven right now on earth. Instead of hiding away from the world and waiting for the rapture to save us, we'd rather think of working in the world to bring about the kingdom wherever God calls us.

KEITH: This is not completely new. Virtually all the early Wesleyan Methodists were post-millennial. They expected the kingdom of God to increase gradually instead of everything getting worse and worse until the ejection effect of the rapture. Then in the twentieth century (after two world wars and boundless inhumanity), most gave up on that approach and adopted pre-millennialism and started looking for escape from a world that was deteriorating. Wesleyans still have not taken a position on the millennium: You can be pre-, post-, or a-millennial and be a Wesleyan. It is interesting to see this kingdom-on-earth view making a comeback among the young.

However, older folk worry that younger folk are eliminating the idea of heaven altogether, as if life here and now is all that matters.

DAVID: It's not eliminated; in a way it becomes more palpable and real. We've heard heaven presented as this big dividing line in history. It starts at some future time, and in the meantime, we're all just sitting around waiting for it. Scripture speaks of the kingdom of heaven being "at hand." For sure, there is a "not yet" to heaven. But there's an "already" to it as well.

KEITH: Theologically that is true. Just be careful in the way you approach these things. It's easy for your heaven-talk to sound out of bounds to older folk.

DAVID: So the problem you have is not that we don't talk about heaven but the way we talk about heaven?

KEITH: It's just not heaven; it is the resurrection too. A person near death needs to know there is more to life than the here and now. That person needs to know that they will live on for eternity, somewhere else or here, but heaven must have a future sense for the dying person, even as it must have a present sense for young people.

DAVID: We're OK with that.

KEITH: Feel free to talk about it then, but don't lose the reality of a future judgment and resurrection or you will have nothing to say to a dying person except to urge them to work harder to establish God's kingdom before they die. It sometimes feels like your generation is open to reevaluating everything. As you reexamine the ideas of the afterlife, keep your eye on orthodox Christian doctrine. Christians believe in "the resurrection of the body and life everlasting." In your urgency to bring the kingdom to pass on earth, don't forget the resurrection and life everlasting. Walk softly.

DAVID: That's a good caution. Perhaps we need to do more "both/and" teaching. Yes, we believe we will spend eternity with Christ in a New Jerusalem. There will be a new heaven and a new earth. But we also believe we must bring the kingdom of God to pass in our world, in the here and now.

KEITH: That'll preach.

DAVID: OK. We need to correct some of our short selling on heaven-talk. I'll agree that we have some work to do here. Peter Kreeft once said that those who believe most strongly in heaven are the ones who made the greatest difference on earth. He may be right. On the other hand, younger generations have speculated on whether all of that difference made on earth was positive. Today the people who believe most strongly in heaven are the Islamic fundamentalist suicide bombers. They will do anything now in order to earn heaven then. The results are horrifying. This kind of belief scares us. We've got to approach it differently.

KEITH: You can't really be comparing us to suicide bombers!

DAVID: Well, not *you*, but our Christian history does include the Crusades. We're wary of any kind of rationalization of current morality because of the heaven trump card.

KEITH: Sure, that's fair. There are excessive and shameful examples and they need avoiding, but do you see my point about keeping the core doctrine of heaven in preaching and teaching?

DAVID: Yes, you're right on that. It's somewhat of an absent message among my generation so far, maybe because we have our whole lives ahead of us and are tired of Christians sitting around waiting to get out of this mess. I think we've got to give more sense to the afterlife in order to give context to this life. Perhaps in our congregations, we can do this hard work as my generation prepares our funeral messages.

KEITH: I'm eager to hear those. Of course, your generation will begin preaching the funeral messages for my generation. You have some time to figure it out, but not much.

DAVID: We'll get on it. So, let's list some questions we should be asking together so we can develop an orthodox theology of heaven and the resurrection that still emphasizes the kingdom of heaven work we have to do today.

Questions for Discussion

1. Do you think heaven has been over-emphasized or under-emphasized?

2. What do you think heaven and the resurrection will be like?

3. As a group, make a list of Scriptures that speak of the afterlife. What do these teach?

4. How do these Scriptures motivate you to change things now?

5. How do these Scriptures reassure you about the future?

6. If our bodies are resurrected like orthodox Christian theology says, what do you think our bodies will be like in the afterlife?

7. Do you think there will be animals—even pets—in heaven? (John Wesley expected his horse to be there.) Defend your answer one way or the other.

8. How can funerals avoid merely celebrating a person's life on earth, but also look forward to the resurrection and the afterlife?

9. As a group, pretend you are a funeral planning committee. What would make a funeral more Christian?

6

Alcohol

We have a glass wine with dinner occasionally; are you telling me we can't do that now if we joined the church?

I heard of a Wesleyan church that actually has board members who drink—that's shameful.

Few things are as damaging to society as alcohol. If it were a new drug we were trying to legalize, it would never get approved.

We need to be defined by what we're, for, not what we're against.

What about other damaging things? Some Wesleyans are addicted to caffeine and overeating, but those aren't banned.

Alcohol has caused more damage to families and society than almost any other drug; people don't beat up their spouse because of an overdose of caffeine.

DAVID: Doesn't it seem like our denomination and others that don't allow drinking alcohol are out of touch?

KEITH: Out of touch with whom? If you mean out of touch with the culture, yes. However, it is not out of touch with our past values and a longstanding stance of most North American evangelicals.

DAVID: Many in my generation wonder what's wrong with a member having a glass of wine with dinner or a casual drink while watching the Super Bowl. Why do Wesleyans make this issue as our "last stand"?

Doesn't it just make our churches an intentionally strange misfit with the culture?

KEITH: It does. Being different than the culture is not a vice in our denomination. Separation from the culture has traditionally been a virtue in the holiness movement.

DAVID: I'm not sure this "virtue" should be considered such a badge of honor. Jesus and the disciples got a lot of flak from the Pharisees about breaking their religious taboos. I suppose that Jesus was different in action and values from the prevailing culture of the time. We should be different from the culture, but so many other ways of difference seem more important to my generation than picking alcohol.

KEITH: Alcohol is just one way. The current way we are different is opposing abortion. The majority of Americans are pro-choice, yet Wesleyans are almost all anti-abortion. We believe the culture is wrong on abortion, and thus we are happy to be different on this stance.

DAVID: Are you saying drinking a glass of wine is like killing a fetus?

KEITH: No, but the comparison helps you younger folk understand our stance on alcohol. The prohibition movement was similar to the anti-abortion movement: It was a vast movement to ban all alcohol from society, and it succeeded for thirteen years from 1920 to 1933. When we eventually lost the fight to completely ban alcohol from society (in 1933), the church's fallback position was to ban alcohol for its own members. There was absolutely unanimous support, just like today's support for the anti-abortion position. Hardly a single person had any other position at the time. The anti-alcohol position was so unanimous that nobody even imagined any other position for most Protestants.

This was not just Wesleyans; the Methodists and many other denominations took the exact same stance too. When prohibition was repealed by the twenty-first amendment, these denominations adopted total abstinence for their own members even though it was legal for the rest of the country. The United Methodist Church still "affirms our long-standing support of abstinence from alcohol as a faithful witness to God's liberating and redeeming love for persons."

DAVID: But things have changed, haven't they?

KEITH: They have. The church has changed too. The practical result of the new Wesleyan "community membership" category is that it permits people who drink to have voting rights in a local church, even if it is argued the intent was to move them closer to the higher standards of the covenant membership commitments.

DAVID: Some larger Wesleyan churches have massive community membership rolls. These members can vote on nearly everything locally and serve in many capacities in the church, but they cannot have "super class A" kind of membership, and they cannot vote to influence the future of the denomination in district and denominational conferences. Over the past few decades, we incrementally made drinking less and less of an issue. Many in my generation wonder if it's time to just drop it altogether and start over with a clean sheet of paper.

KEITH: True, some gradually softened their stance on alcohol. Evangelicals became the majority church in America as the former mainline churches diminished. As Wesleyans increasingly identified themselves as Evangelicals, they increasingly have been influenced by other evangelical institutions, colleges, and denominations, who have softened their requirements for total abstinence for members or staff.

DAVID: One of my generation's chief concerns is our integrity on the alcohol issue. Many churches practice a "don't ask, don't tell" policy on drinking. Some pastors say, "We probably have many members and leaders who drink, but we don't make a big fuss about it, so we don't know." Isn't this a problem of authenticity? It is dishonest to expect people to make a promise they won't keep. It is a matter of integrity to many in my generation. Many of us would rather change the rule than have this "wink-wink, don't ask, don't tell" practice.

KEITH: Wesleyans don't have church rules, they are membership commitments—commitments that members make to each other. These aren't rules dreamed up by the headquarters, but commitments all Wesleyans together have decided to bind on ourselves, like a family agrees on the ground rules of a household. They have changed tremendously over time as new generations of Wesleyans drop old ones and add new ones. We used to expect each other to commit to not buying anything on Sunday or to completely abstain from dancing, but those expectations have changed as the collective convictions of Wesleyans changed. Until an item changes, there is tension (as there now is on the alcohol issue). Some live by their commitments and others ignore them until enough folk believe a change should be made, and that can happen at any General Conference—several each decade.

DAVID: But the integrity issue remains. I know of one church plant that actually left the denomination over this. When they began to do membership classes and realized they couldn't be authentic to The Wesleyan Church membership commitments, they left. They felt like in order to be Wesleyan they needed to be true to that. Rather than practice wink-wink leadership or try to change things, they just left. Other church plants adjust their structure so only a handful of their people are full-fledged covenant members and no one else even knows about the drinking commitment. That seems like a recipe for disaster. Wouldn't it be more honest to change the rule, or rather the commitments?

KEITH: I have a different take on this. I think these churches are the ones making alcohol the big issue. Have these people truly examined the membership commitments honestly? Or have they just glanced through and picked a few items to wave their integrity flag over? For instance, what about the rest of the membership commitments? Where is all their concern about integrity for those? On the same list are commitments to give to the needy; have family devotions; have personal devotions; practice fasting; give food to hungry people; give clothing to the destitute; visit people who are sick; visit people in prison; and respect individual rights regardless of race, color, or sex. All these are on the same list as alcohol! Why aren't they making more cries about integrity over these commitments which many of their members fail to keep?

DAVID: These are all good things we hope every member will do. My generation doesn't get as worked up about people falling short of visiting the sick because everyone thinks they should. But many of my generation think a church has no right to tell its members what they can't do unless the Bible is absolutely clear on it. It is what *The Discipline* bans that the Bible doesn't forbid that bothers us.

KEITH: Well the commitments come up for grabs at every general conference. The way we've set up the church is to grant a vote to those who have gone before us by requiring the present voters to agree before a commitment can be changed. If the voters don't agree it should be changed, it stands. It only takes a vote of Wesleyans today to overturn the vote of the last hundred years, and that can be done at any general conference. To young people it may seem unfair that past members have such a strong say in the present. Nevertheless, as

Wesleyans, we've followed the constitutional model—where it can be changed. But until it is changed, it stands. When you really look at it, our predecessors provided a way for any generation to overturn past views through this process.

DAVID: So it is engagement with the process of district and general conferences that may be the route to change. You brought up abortion as an example to compare with the alcohol issue. As *The Discipline* now stands, there is no "covenant membership commitment" on abortion at all, just an advisory statement. Yet we expect a commitment of those covenant members to not drink. Perhaps we need to reverse these positions—advise people on drinking and require them to be anti-abortion? Maybe we need to get into more of a routine of examining these commitments at every general conference. New "temptations" become popular and need to be added. Old "temptations" become, in reality, less serious as time passes.

KEITH: Which is another reason why churches or individuals need not leave the denomination over this issue. It's only one issue in *The Discipline*; we should work together to make our commitments reflect God's guidance on our common collective convictions today. The commitments aren't established by headquarters. They are made by the elected delegates to general conference; they can be changed by vote.

DAVID: I wonder if your rosy view of church politics with no backroom meetings is the reality. The conferences I have attended seemed to play out as well-scripted plays, based on the "meetings before the meeting."

Maybe there is a larger question here. Should we be asking, "Why offer membership at all?" Is membership necessary in order to be the church? More problems than solutions seem to be caused by membership rules. Doesn't membership draw lines between people, calling some "in" and others "out"? Maybe the idea of membership itself is antiquated.

KEITH: The idea of doing away with membership is not new in the holiness movement. One of our sister denominations, the Church of God-Anderson was founded in 1881, with no formal membership at all. It still has no formal membership. Wesleyans could do that too, if they redesigned *The Discipline* to reflect that approach. It could be started at any general conference.

It is hard to argue, though, that the early church had no membership or no membership rules. If we seriously wanted to follow the pattern of the second hundred years of church history, we'd raise the standards of membership, not lower them. And we'd delay new member's entry into the church for several years while they prepared. To boot, during their time of preparation they would be dismissed before any communion service, because they would not be able to take communion until they were baptized, and they could not be baptized until after several years of training. That approach might have worked when there was only one "denomination" in the world. In today's world, it would seem strange.

We have adopted less stringent standards for membership today, and even those change over time. There are a dozen things that were rules when I was your age that are gone now, and new ones have been added. I expect your generation will do the same, and I expect you'll add some new ones. When you add something (like we added the anti-abortion advisory in 1984), you will virtually all agree on it at the time, just like they agreed on alcohol for more than a century, and like we mostly all agree on abortion now. Then your children later might think your rule is goofy and they'll push against it and want to drop it. They'll call your commitments "legalism."

DAVID: OK, I see your point. In a local church board meeting recently, we asked the question, "What would it take for us to remove someone from our membership roll?" If a member in our church opened up a strip club in town, would we remove him? The obvious answer was yes, so there is a line, and we continued with a discussion as to where that line should be. It was a good (although strange) hypothetical start to the discussion.

KEITH: Exactly. It is interesting how the membership commitments work in real life. It is easier to use the membership commitments to keep a person from getting in than use them to kick a member out. There seems to be (in actual life) more patience with a member not up to par with the commitments than there is with new members coming in. The biblical stance of the apostle Paul is concern for the church body and the reputation it has in the community. That may be why Paul was so vehement on expelling the man sleeping with his father's wife in Corinth.

DAVID: My generation has its own list too, but I think our list will have more positive actions we expect members to do rather than things we disallow, especially things that don't have direct biblical support.

KEITH: So be it. Your generation shall have your own chance to revise the list and make your own. That is how this denomination is set up. We have no papacy and even our *Articles of Religion* can be amended by two-thirds vote and ratification. My generation (and the one immediately before us) made massive changes in 1968, when the Pilgrim Holiness and Wesleyan Methodist denominations merged to become The

Wesleyan Church. All kinds of things got tossed out and new things were introduced. We have steadily made changes ever since. Your generation is coming up to bat now, and you can do the same. But in order to make changes you'll have to be engaged in the conversation instead of running off on your own to make your own mini-denomination-of-one-church, like the church plant you mentioned. The Wesleyan Church is founded on democratic principles. Any time the people want to change things, they can do so by vote.

DAVID: So, how should we approach the issue of alcohol in the future? What message do the older generations have for the younger ones about drinking and membership?

KEITH: We worry that the emerging generations want to be too much like the world; they want to fit in with unbelievers instead of being willing to be different from the world. Some of us were raised in churches where homes were wrecked by alcohol; women were beaten by drunken husbands who had spent the grocery money on alcohol. Some of us think the world would be a better place if there were no alcohol at all. Our own parents failed to make that happen in prohibition. Some of us wonder if you will only subtract and never add to *The Discipline*, melting away all prohibitions so that anything goes in the future church.

DAVID: So, what should a younger local church pastor do about membership and drinking in the meantime? How do we effectively lead, yet not sell out? If the trajectory of this discussion seems to point toward change, what do we do in the mean time? Should we let our new members in on the sly, whispering to them that this will probably change? Or should we hold the standards with full integrity until it changes, if it does actually change in the future?

KEITH: I think for now, whatever the intent, the community membership in The Wesleyan Church provides all any honest pastor needs if he or she wants to provide involvement for people who won't give up their glass of wine with dinner. I may not like it much, but it is a fact.

Wesleyan delegates at a general conference created a new level of local church membership for people who do not follow the full membership commitments. These members have extensive rights regarding voting and involvement in the local church. If they are not willing to give up their glass of wine to become full members, I wonder why they are valuing their glass of wine more than full membership. If wine is an issue for them, then why do they want to be full members?

Wesleyans have never taught that church membership is the same as being a Christian. We've always believed a person can be a Christian and not be a member of any church. Wesleyans recognize there are all kinds of Christians who don't practice what we value. Our membership commitments represent what we value collectively. That list changes over time, and your generation will probably subtract from that list and add to it too.

This is why it is important for your generation to quit thinking your parents are making curfew rules for you. The denomination includes your generation, and you can do your homework and persuade the rest of us of what you think the membership commitments should be. If your generation wants the membership commitments to reflect your own convictions, you have to get elected as a delegate or you will end up letting all us old folk make all these decisions for you. That's my advice. So, as a member of the coming generation, what suggestions do you have for us older folk on this issue?

DAVID: We need some of you to be guardian angels or allies in our attempts to make this our own denomination. You changed things. Help us know how to change things too. Don't freeze in your own changes saying, "This far and no more." We hope you'll advocate for some younger people for district positions and elect some younger folk as delegates. Help us understand how conferences work and how to prepare resolutions that actually change things. Help us move from complaining to changing. Talk with us about the issues (like you and I are doing here), so we can figure out the good things we need to keep and which things we should toss out. Warn us when we want to go too far, and scold us when we complain instead of trying to change things. Understand that while we want to make changes just like you did, we don't want to destroy all the good things you've passed on to us. We just want to make a better church to do God's work in the present age, not in the past ages.

KEITH: OK, this is a sticky issue. Most everyone already has his or her mind made up. A loving, low-temperature discussion is hard to come by in this topic of conversation. Some in my generation think it is not even proper to discuss this. So, let's try to list some questions here that younger and older folk could talk together about on this subject to bring us all closer.

Questions for Discussion

1. What changes have you seen in church membership commitments during your lifetime?

2. How did these things change?

3. What were some of the good changes in your opinion? Bad changes?

4. What were some of the expectations years ago that weren't even written down but were still expected of all serious church members?

5. What is the purpose of membership commitments?

6. What is the purpose of membership itself? What do you think of the no-membership idea?

7. Where would you draw the line on refusing to accept a new member?

8. What would it take to get a member expelled from your church? Has it ever happened? How?

9. If your group were making membership commitments for the entire denomination on blank paper, what would you require?

10. Do you think a full member should be able to drink a glass of wine with a meal? If so, how many? Scripture condemns drunkenness— how would drinkers know they have crossed this line? How is your position rooted in the Bible's teaching?

11. Do you think that all membership commitments should be directly tied to Scripture? If so, what is your view on pornography or legal marijuana use (as it is in some states and countries)? What other things do you think are wrong, yet there is no specific verse about them in the Bible?

12. Does a denomination have a right to make membership requirements? Why or why not?

7

Sanctification

I can't remember the last time I heard a message on holiness in my "holiness movement" church.

What does sanctification really mean? Aren't we really in danger of being like a cult if our view is so rare among other Christians?

I don't have a problem talking about becoming more holy like the Scriptures say—I just have a problem with the holier than thou types.

Have we abandoned our doctrine of sanctification? Do we even believe this anymore?

Too many of the young ministers these days don't even really believe in entire sanctification.

The only testimonies I hear now are confessions of sin—why don't we have victory-over-sin testimonies?

I've been a Wesleyan all my life—and I've never really understood what sanctification is. What is it?

KEITH: The Wesleyan Church has been preaching entire sanctification for years, but I don't hear much holiness preaching from the emerging generations. Are we losing a central truth of our tradition and becoming just like every other evangelical denomination?

DAVID: I'm not sure you can blame our generation for abandoning holiness. It was your generation, the boomers, who abandoned preaching entire sanctification, or at least changed the way it was preached so few could recognize it.

KEITH: Ouch!

DAVID: Sorry. The truth may hurt. When I was growing up, the church was preoccupied with evangelism and church growth more than holiness. Your generation made fun of the "small but pure" mentality—using jokes like "us four and no more" to mock the small churches. You were trying to go from good to great, or maybe from goodness to greatness—and by greatness, you meant more people, more buildings, more excellence, and most of all, more attendance. Your generation switched to using the word *evangelical* to define Wesleyan more than *holiness.* You can't pin the decline of holiness preaching on us. It seems to me we are the generation trying to rediscover it—albeit in a way you might not recognize.

KEITH: Maybe some in my generation did abandon holiness preaching, but we were trying to correct what we thought were excesses in the past—like legalism, narrow-mindedness, and lack of evangelistic fervor.

DAVID: Maybe your generation tossed out the baby with the bathwater.

KEITH: Perhaps we did, but there are still many Wesleyans who hold holy living in high esteem. Many of us believe God can purify a Christian in a second work of grace.

DAVID: Your generation may believe these things, but they don't talk or preach about them much. Most of us in the younger generations have rarely heard a personal testimony to entire sanctification. Your generation has held on to this distinctive mostly by inspecting the doctrine of ministerial candidates. Many ministers my age heard more about holiness when we interviewed with the ordination committee than we had in several years of listening to preaching.

Actually I think many younger preachers in our denomination preach holiness stronger than most boomer preachers. We're hearing it from other corners of the church too. Just last week I even heard a podcast message from Mark Driscoll on the "Be ye holy" portion of 1 Peter. Those twenty minutes contained more forceful preaching on the doctrine of holiness than I ever heard growing up in Wesleyan churches.

KEITH: You're kidding me! Driscoll is such a five-point Calvinist, sometimes I wonder if he would like to add two more points.

DAVID: Yep, surprised me too. That's the shift I'm talking about. The message went dormant for a while but is sprouting up in unlikely places. When I heard preaching on holiness growing up, there was so much emphasis on what it didn't mean, I hardly ever heard what it did mean. Younger holiness preachers in my generation simply proclaim that God can deliver Christians from sinful habits through spiritual power. They seem to take the Bible at face value on this one.

KEITH: My generation did spend a lot of time explaining what holiness isn't; after all, we carry a lot of baggage from the past. However, your younger preachers should be able to communicate the core idea of holiness—there is power from God to enable us to be what He calls us to be. Holiness is not trying to live right, it is trusting God to give the changing grace of deliverance and empowerment.

DAVID: I think the more we study the Scriptures, the more the younger generations are inclined toward holiness, even those outside of the traditional holiness camp. I am not sure, though, that we expect spiritual transformation to happen as quickly or easily as we've sometimes heard it outlined from our doctrinal inspectors.

KEITH: We accept that, though reluctantly. It does seem like God is working more slowly with the emerging generation—even with our own generation today. Our own parents preached that at a single moment, a person could be totally cleansed and sanctified and live victoriously from then on. My generation still believed this was possible, just not common. Your generation seems to have made it rare.

DAVID: Many in the emerging generation are definitely "longer way" types. The key word you used is *could*. God could do this work in an instant. However, when our parents had marriage problems, they were sent to counseling instead of the altar. When people confessed to addictions, they were urged to slap on nicotine patches or join recovery groups. We didn't invent these longer paths to recovery; the boomers introduced them. Change that works well seems to take longer to us too. Then of course, there is the opposite problem of the boomers. Rather than seeking change at the altar, or even a counselor or support group, they just sought divorce lawyers! The longer way has often felt like the most authentic way to many in our generation.

KEITH: I admit this. We believed that God could do his work in us immediately, but he didn't always do so; thus we provided slower routes to recovery and cleansing, along with the altar call deliverance. That's not new. The old time holiness preachers always preached, "Seek until you receive." Seeking is not a shorter way; it allows for a period of seeking, sometimes for years.

DAVID: This is why your generation surrendered the idea of deliverance to the charismatic movement, right?

KEITH: Interesting thought. Indeed, in the 1970s, most Wesleyans rejected the charismatic movement as too emotional and extravagant. At the time, we were trying to become more respectable and less wacky ourselves. You are probably fair in charging us with abandoning ship on instant deliverance. But we still believed it was possible—at least we kept it on the books.

DAVID: Yeah, but The United Methodist Church still has the same thing on the books—a solid doctrine of "Christian perfection."

KEITH: True, what is written down is not enough. OK, I sound defensive here, but given that my generation gravitated away from emphasizing instant cleansing, I'm wondering where your generation will come out on the call to holiness. How will your preachers address the Bible's call to holy living?

DAVID: Dr. Steve Lennox once said that movements are defined by how they answer certain questions. He then listed a few questions and described how he thought Wesleyans would answer them. His final question was, "How saved can we be?"

KEITH: I remember that. He said our answer to the question is that we can be saved fully and completely and that there is no limit to God's grace. I should also point out that Lennox is one of those boomers you're talking about.

DAVID: You've got me there! I think that his question, "How saved can we be?" is a compelling question for younger generations. The holiness movement naturally tilts toward an optimism of grace. On a theological level, for my generation, it seems like instant heresy when someone tries to limit God. You'll often hear people say, "God certainly can do anything—you'll never hear me say he can't." This is the open door through which a reemphasized and re-imagined doctrine of sanctification can emerge among my generation.

KEITH: I'm OK with reemphasizing, but I wonder what you mean by *re-imagined*. It seems every time a younger writer grapples with an orthodox doctrine, they have to re-imagine it.

DAVID: I understand your caution there, but to re-imagine is to light a fire of passion under the original ideas. It's to dream in our own minds what the doctrine could mean. When we re-imagine, we collectively admit that we haven't fully followed and realized truth, and that it likely covers more aspects of life than we assumed. This involves confession and progression.

KEITH: Yes, we need to do that. You've established pretty well that my generation hasn't fully taught (or lived out) our sanctification doctrine as we could. But, what progression do you all have in mind?

DAVID: Well, I've noticed there is a lot of discussion, preaching, and writing about the process of sanctification—the steps or order of how it works in the believer's life. How it happens has been the key.

KEITH: Yes, there are numerous views of sanctification among evangelicals. Theologian Chris Bounds and I wrote a paper on the "Seven Approaches to Holiness" that included a broad span.[1]

DAVID: Right, I remember that. Remind me of that list again if you will.

KEITH: The first is the "Holiness of Christ—not me" approach. This is the most pessimistic approach. All you can do is confess your constant sinfulness and trust the holiness of Christ. Next is the "Worthy goal—but impossible dream" approach, which means followers of Christ should try for the goal of holiness, but nobody will actually reach it.

DAVID: How depressing! My generation is too optimistic about God's power for that.

KEITH: Next are those who consider holiness "A momentary experience—but unsustainable." Then there are those who consider holiness to be "A sustainable experience—with momentary lapses." These approaches see the holy life as including many mountain peaks and valleys.

DAVID: I can see why many approach holiness this way. Life sure seems like that when you take in the big picture.

KEITH: But many believe (and I'm among them) that it doesn't have to be that way. That's where the next three approaches come from. Next, there are those who believe holiness is "Possible—but only after a long growth process," also known as the "longer way." This means that after a long journey, maybe lasting decades, you can get off the roller coaster and have a steady, faithful life of holiness without lapses of sin.

DAVID: Yes, I've seen people like this too. Of course they were never prideful about it; they didn't wear their holiness like a medal on their chest. They wore it in humility and with an earnest desire to keep learning from the Master.

KEITH: Sure, that's how all responses to God's work should be. What's more, some approaches are even more optimistic. There is the view that you can "Keep seeking until you receive," known as the "middle way." This means that, while the timeline is indefinite, if you seek diligently and prepare your heart in a season of holy searching, then you can receive entire sanctification in an instant. Finally there are those that say you can "Believe and receive by faith now." This is the "shorter way" popularized by Phoebe Palmer. This most optimistic view treats sanctification much like salvation. In other words, nothing should hold you back from receiving this work of grace right now, just like when you received salvation.

DAVID: That's helpful to see those views strung together. The last two are the ones we seem to have lost in the last few decades. I can count on one hand the number of times I've heard a compelling call at the end of a message based on either of the final two views—and still have fingers left over.

KEITH: Yes, some of us grieve that loss. It is partially a result of the general pessimism of the prevailing worldview. Those last two approaches are how it was preached almost exclusively in the holiness movement of the past, and now the pendulum seems to be swinging.

DAVID: Those were the days, I suppose. It is hard for me to criticize a call to commitment I have not really heard much.

KEITH: Maybe some in your generation will study the holiness texts in Scripture and offer one of these last two approaches again. Maybe you will see some really transformed lives—even in an instant!

DAVID: Yes, that would be wonderful. And my peers will likely think they've reinvented the wheel.

KEITH: As long as it happens, I'll be happy. However, speaking of reinvention, how do you think the younger generations will approach all this?

DAVID: I don't know if you'll like it, but I don't think we'll be focusing on the how much at all.

KEITH: What do you mean?

DAVID: All the wonderful approaches you just outlined deal with the vertical—the "How much can you be saved?" question. What I am seeing is a re-imagination of sanctification in horizontal terms: "How much can the world be saved?"

KEITH: I think I see where you are heading with that.

DAVID: Holiness as re-imagined today involves more than just personal holiness. Many younger folk are now emphasizing other dynamics. Your seven approaches, as well as the four views of sanctification Chris Bounds delivered at a general conference, have to do with a personal journey of holiness. There is also a corporate call to holiness, where God sanctifies the body of Christ. The "be ye holy" is more of "y'all be holy." This call is to the entire church, not just individuals.

KEITH: That's where membership commitments came from. They are an attempt to make the church more like God's vision for the world.

DAVID: Yes, but the emphasis so far has always been on these two dynamics of holiness: the personal pursuit and the corporate commitment. They are only half of the plan. There are four dynamics of holiness.[2]

KEITH: So, where do the other two lead us?

DAVID: Relational holiness. So much emphasis has been put on personal and corporate holiness commitments that we often overlook relational holiness. My generation is far more sensitive to relational sin. How one treats other people is viewed as the vital evidence of holiness. Unfortunately, the corporate membership commitments have been used to beat people over the head. In an ironic twist, some people have fought against the corporate holiness dynamic because they have a higher sensitivity to relational holiness. I think this is because of a lack of balance. God wants the older generations to learn the *allelon* commitments of Scripture again, those "one another" commands. And the younger generations will, in time, find the power of corporate commands.

KEITH: I see what you're saying. In fact, you might say that all the "what I'm not saying about holiness" messages you criticized earlier were our boomer attempts to change the way we talk about holiness to be more relational.

DAVID: Perhaps that's where we started learning it and why it's such a key value for us—but it doesn't stop there. The other part is missional holiness. Younger preachers emphasize this fourth dynamic a great deal. You might not recognize a particular sermon as being about holiness, but the younger generations believe holiness involves changing the world, not just each other and ourselves. We are not satisfied with a holy person or even a holy church—we want a holy world.

KEITH: Of course, the history of the holiness movement includes a rich emphasis on the transformation of the world. Wesley's Methodist revival famously resulted in the closing of bars for lack of patrons, the jails for lack of criminals, and orphanages for lack of the abandoned.

DAVID: Sure, this wheel was not invented by us, but the tide is rising again on this fourth wave of holiness. When we speak of justice and helping the poor, we include reaching the neighborhood for Christ, but we also include the problems of human trafficking and AIDS. These issues are not merely elements of evangelism or service; they are core elements of holiness. We believe God is in the business of sanctifying us so that we might join him in sanctifying the world.

KEITH: I think that's a re-imagination and reemphasis on holiness that would do us good. However, I hope that as you upgrade the relational and world-sanctifying elements of holiness, you don't forget personal and corporate holiness. Generations often drop the first half of truth in their effort to emphasize the other half of truth.

DAVID: We do need to remember that. Sanctifying the world without considering the sanctification of individuals would be just as great an imbalance as sanctifying individuals and forgetting the world. How do you think our two generations could come together on holiness to move ahead to the future? How can we bring a balanced embrace of holiness and an optimistic view of the grace of God back to the forefront? What questions do the generations in local churches need to discuss together now?

KEITH: Let's make our list right now.

Questions for Discussion

1. What are the seven vertical approaches to holiness that various denominations embrace to answer the question, "How saved can you be?" See if you can list them and explain each as a group.

2. Which of the seven approaches have you heard people talk about the most? Which view do you lean toward yourself?

3. How could we introduce the more optimistic views to people in an authentic way?

4. What are the four horizontal dynamics of holiness which answer the question, "How saved can the world be?" List them as a group.

5. Which of the four dynamics of holiness are you most passionate about and what are you doing about it these days?

6. What other words for *sanctification* have you heard people use? Which do you like and dislike? Why?

7. What Scriptures have you encountered that talk about holiness and help answer the questions, "How saved can you be?" and "How saved can the world be?"

8. What kind of preaching on sanctification did you hear years ago? What have you heard more recently?

9. How does the general ethos of culture's pessimism or optimism affect what people believe about sanctification?

10. When was the last time you heard a personal testimony about deliverance from a sin? Entire sanctification? Is there one you'd be willing to give now?

Notes

1. Chris Bounds and Keith Drury, "Seven Approaches to Holiness," http://www.drurywriting.com/keith/holiness.positions.htm (accessed March 23, 2009).
2. David Drury, "Four Dynamics of Holiness" (speech, Christian Holiness Association, Lansing, Mich., 2008).

8

Women in Leadership

I'm fine with ordaining women—but I wouldn't want a woman preacher at our church every week.

Let's look for a woman for this role. Anyone know one to nominate?

How come we ordain women when the Bible says they shouldn't even speak in church?

Half the people in this church came from a denomination that doesn't ordain women. It's going to be hard for them to swallow.

Why do we have a "token woman" on all our committees?

My daughter is called into the ministry and graduated at the top of her class. How come no church will hire her for an actual ministry job?

DAVID: Dad, why do Wesleyans have so few women in leadership? Seems like there are many who study for the ministry or feel called but few end up in pastoral positions.

KEITH: We used to have a lot of women ministers; some argue there were periods when as many as a third of our ministers were women.

DAVID: Sure, we have some good history stories, and I have heard them. But I'm speaking about now. I've never seen a strong representation in our leadership and in our actual churches. I can't name one mid-to-large size Wesleyan church that has a woman as senior pastor, for instance. I hope I'm wrong; perhaps there are some I don't know about.

KEITH: You are right. There are fewer now than we once had, but we do have a strong history of women preachers. The sermon for the very first ordination of a woman in America was preached by a Wesleyan Methodist minister. From the beginning (except for a short time when we wobbled), Wesleyan Methodists ordained women. From the beginning, the other half of our grand-parentage—the Pilgrim Holiness Church—has ordained women continually. Yes, the number of women ministers did decline after World War II. However, we have ordained women all along.

DAVID: I suppose this feels like one of those "on the books but not on our hearts" issues. Why is that? We keep bumping into this kind of problem. Wesleyans seem to have been ahead of the times on many issues in our history, but when you get to the present we are often behind the times.

KEITH: It does appear that way, but we have always ordained women who claimed a call to preach and those who opposed ordaining women have always been in the minority (except for a short time more than a hundred year ago).

DAVID: If we believe in ordaining women pastors, then why aren't there more women pastors? Isn't it virtually useless to ordain women if there are not jobs for them in churches?

KEITH: Well, it isn't completely useless, but it is certainly awkward. We ordain men who don't always find jobs too. On this issue, Wesleyans sometimes face a conflict of competing values. Wesleyans value ordaining women, but we also value local congregational power. We have empowered local churches to decide whom they hire as their ministers. If we had an Episcopal system of church government, where denominational leaders "appoint" ministers in churches despite the local members' preferences, I bet we'd have a lot more ministerial jobs for women. However, we have chosen to let local churches decide whom they will employ as their pastor, so the woman minister (or male minister) has to get voted on to get the job. The truth is that many local churches prefer male ministers. Thus, women who are even more gifted than their male counterparts sometimes don't get jobs as pastors, because the church sticks to their preferences in electing a pastor.

DAVID: Isn't *preferences* just another word for *prejudices*?

KEITH: Probably. Even though denominational leaders have regularly supported women as ministers, local church members are influenced by other perspectives too. A significant number of evangelical denominations (along with the entire Roman Catholic church) refuse ordination to women on what they consider biblical grounds, so when people transfer into Wesleyan churches they often bring these views with them. Wesleyan leaders have a hard time persuading them differently. Even some lifelong Wesleyans read books and listen to preachers with these views and are reluctant to have a women minister.

DAVID: I've bumped into that in my own church. A search team I was leading was looking for a new youth pastor. One team member said, "When we hire him"—speaking about whoever might be brought on the staff. I slipped in a small correction, adding, ". . . or her."

He stopped abruptly, shook his head, and insisted, "No, him."

I replied again the same way (as the tension in the meeting rose) by inserting, ". . . or *her*."

Frustrated with my resistance to his statement, this boomer leader in our church then got on his soapbox. He said, "I could see having a woman in leadership in some other role, but here we're talking about working with teenagers, and the pastor needs to have authority with them. That's why we need a man in this role." I think he was staking a claim since we already have women in leadership in our pastoral staff, and I had pointed out before his speech that the Wesleyan church ordains women, so his position was out of line. What's more, half the committee was made up of women, including his own wife. He wasn't going to give in no matter what was "on the books" among Wesleyans.

KEITH: So what happened?

DAVID: I gave him the benefit of the doubt, saying, "Perhaps you just haven't seen a woman ministering to teens with authority." I then gave an example: "My sister-in-law is a Wesleyan youth pastor right now and has preached here at our church to more than a thousand people. She has a pretty commanding presence, and I think if you saw her in leadership, you might change your mind." Then someone else on the committee recommended that he should read Ken Schenk's helpful booklet entitled *What Wesleyans Believe About Women in Ministry.* The meeting moved on and he did not say anything else about that issue.

KEITH: Where did all this end up?

DAVID: I give the guy a lot of credit; he has a lot of character and teachability. About five days later, he e-mailed me: "Dave, I did my homework since that meeting. I was wrong. I'll fully support it if a woman is our best candidate."

KEITH: It's nice to have a good ending on a discussion like that. Unfortunately, many similar discussions in the church don't turn out so well.

DAVID: I'm sure that's true. I think many in the younger generations are frustrated when they see people publicly assent to the written statements of the denomination and then privately or behind closed doors push back on women in ministry. It's hypocritical. Aren't women equal persons with all the rights men have? Why do we still have to work so hard to champion this?

KEITH: Yes, I teach young people, and they are almost universal in their agreement with what you say here. Their position is pro-women-in-ministry "on the books" (or in their talk) but I really don't see it in their actions any more than among older folk. I see the speakers the younger generation invites to conventions, conferences, and youth camps, and it appears to me the emerging generation doesn't walk their talk any better than the older folk. They're always putting younger *men* in these slots. In fact, I would argue older folk have done more to favor women as speakers and leaders than your own generation. Remember, it was mostly older folk who elected the first woman General Superintendent and the first woman college president in The Wesleyan Church.

DAVID: Ouch! You're right on that. Your generation has made great progress—both at the top and at the bottom. Women are included at the highest level leadership positions, as well as having equality in ministerial training and maybe even in entry-level staff positions. But the middle is the challenge—local board positions for lay women and district superintendent or senior pastor positions for the ordained. Here's where your generation looks the other way rather than confronting the prejudice when you've sensed it or even heard it expressed outright.

KEITH: I admit we do better placing women on committees and boards at the general conference level than we do as senior pastors. We've done much better with the appointed positions than the elected ones. Some churches still have an "understanding" that board members should be male, but this seems to be changing. Women make up 60–65 percent of our members who tithe. It is difficult for a church to continue to refuse to elect people from a group that constitutes a majority of its members and financial supporters. When few women had income and the tithe was based on the husband's salary, it may have been easier to overlook women. That is simply not true today.

DAVID: Even that explanation rubs me wrong. Why should it matter where the majority of the tithes come from? Why overlook a woman leader, or a potential leader from another race or economic level, just because they aren't representing a large enough block of givers? Should our leaders be selected on a *quid pro quo* basis? It sounds a little corrupt to me.

KEITH: Of course, it is not fair, but it has often been true. Thankfully, it is less true recently. I just mean that as women have grown in their influence and earning power, reality sets in for some people. Like it or not, the church sometimes takes its cues from culture.

DAVID: That's exactly the problem younger generations are trying to point out—the church should be counter-cultural on these things, and I think we can all expend some leadership energy to ensure we involve women in leadership.

KEITH: So you younger folk are taking over the church soon. Indeed, you already make up a growing part of the voters at district and general conference. What do you expect from us older folk in your own quest to make room for more women in ministry and leadership?

DAVID: We all need to get better at supporting women leaders in a general way, but even more to the point, we need to learn to be personally eager to hear a woman preach in our church, to lead our district, to be on the board, and to be in charge. We need to be aware that women called to preach often deal with an arbitrary ceiling; we need to remove the barriers and eliminate the prejudice.

KEITH: I think we're doing that on many levels, just maybe not enough.

DAVID: So what would you say to us younger people who are impatient at the progress of women who are called to the ministry?

KEITH: First, I'd say you should stick with your conviction that God calls both men and women to ministry. Don't capitulate to the fundamentalist and Catholic approach that reserves ministry for only males. Then, I would say, "persuade, don't dictate." Mostly people are persuaded on things like this. Ramming things down their throats usually causes pushback.

I also hope you will raise up the women ministers and leaders from your own generation. Be willing to elect them to leadership positions and to offer them prominent speaking opportunities. When you find a young woman leader, promote her in the church, and elect her to roles of responsibility. As women are given the opportunity to preach and lead, gradually people will see that God honors their ministry, and they will become increasingly open to a woman pastor for their own church.

Finally, give us some credit for what our generation has accomplished. Our denominational leaders and district superintendents are unanimous on this, even if the percentage of women in roles of leadership is still smaller than it should be. Increasingly the ball is in your court. You can make it so a woman minister is no longer a rare exception. It is your turn soon. We provided the opening for women ministers on the books; you don't have to change that. We have made some progress. Now you can fill up the pulpits.

DAVID: I admit we've got some work to do on this one, especially among youth ministers. I see what you are saying about using the points of influence we already have to make a difference here and now—not just assuming it's your problem. What else should we encourage both generations to discuss in their local church? Let's make a list.

Questions for Discussion

1. Why do you think some churches and denominations refuse to ordain women?

2. What advice would you give your daughter or granddaughter if she told you she was sure God was calling her into the ministry?

3. Who are the women leaders in your own local church and what kind of role do they play?

4. Who were the women leaders in the Bible that are models of female leadership?

5. List each of the standards for elders and ministers listed in Titus 1 and 1 Timothy 3, and then ask how we use these standards for ministers today in our own church.

6. What are some of the disadvantages a male minister has as a pastor? What are the disadvantages a female pastor has?

7. What are some of the advantages a male minister has as a pastor? What are the advantages a female pastor has?

8. What do we miss out on if all our preaching comes from males? What would we miss out on if all our preaching came from females?

9. Some women pastors say they actually get more resistance from women in the church than from males. Why might this be true?

10. How has the role of the preacher's wife changed over the years, and how does this change relate to this discussion?

9

Denominational Leadership

I'm not sure our leaders understand what it's like on the front lines.

Why do we even need a denomination? Shouldn't the church be decentralized?

Churches don't appreciate leaders until a crisis comes along. When they rescue the situation, we are relieved and see the need.

I'm more influenced by large church pastors and independent publishing houses than my denominational leaders.

We need strong leadership for the future of the denomination—we need them to tell us where we are going. We don't get that.

Our leaders are there for a reason, I guess, but we don't bother them and we hope they won't bother us.

DAVID: Many of us younger folk think that the higher someone climbs in leadership, the more out of touch they get.

KEITH: Now we've hit upon a subject that I think my generation really did invent.

DAVID: What—being out of touch?

KEITH: No, rebellion against authority. We thought the same way about leaders in the church before we took over. Many still think this way about our own boomer leaders, no matter who they are.

DAVID: But your generation is running everything. You took over early and have a death grip on virtually every local church and denominational position out there.

KEITH: Yes, we did take over quickly, for two reasons. First, the generation before us—the so-called "silent generation" that was born immediately before and during World War II—was so few in number. The church needed us to fill leadership spots earlier than previous generations. In a way, leadership skipped a generation, so we took over early. When the generation before—those who fought in World War II—reached their sixties and seventies, they lost control and we took over fast. The second reason is there were *lots* of us—the boomers were the largest generation North America had ever seen. When we were dissatisfied, we did something about it. We quickly took over leadership and changed things.

DAVID: Well, good for you guys! Take a moment, boomers everywhere, to pat yourselves on the back. I know your generation is good at that. Perhaps we should create awards for the records of longevity being set everywhere. We'll etch on them: "Got church power early and held on forever!"

KEITH: OK, Mr. Sarcasm. You got me a little sidetracked there. I was only pointing out that my generation wasn't too trusting of the generations before us either. We questioned authority and worked hard until we got authority.

DAVID: Yes, I've heard that. I've even heard some people claim the attitudes of the younger generations today are a typical "phase" the young go through. But I think it's deeper than that.

KEITH: Upon reflection, I agree. Your generation—I'm thinking of those born in the '70s and '80s, not those in college now—sometimes seems bitter or dismissive of leaders. They stand on the sidelines expecting our generation to change things for them. Nobody changed things for us—we did the changing ourselves. The criticism of leadership from your generation can sometimes be brutal. Why is that?

DAVID: Young adults today have a deeper distrust of leaders, because we feel like we're the first generation in America to inherit a worse world than the generations before us. We have seen a multitude of boomer leaders fall spiritually, even though they were "great leaders." And we're getting the short end of the economic stick—we expect to have a lower standard of living than our parents. We have been given broken homes, broken economies, broken churches, and broken promises. I agree that a bitter or dismissive response is not the most constructive response, but it is a reality among many in my generation.

KEITH: My generation knows rebellion and revolution. We were the ones who took over the church and changed almost everything. What we don't understand is a generation who gets bitter about leadership. We'd understand it better if you all organized a block of votes and elected one of your own. That's what we did. It seems to us that some younger folk act victimized by entrenched leadership. We think they ought to revolt and elect their own instead of crawling under the stairs and pouting.

The real question may be what we can do about the dismissive attitude, victimization, and even (in some cases) bitterness among the younger generations. Maybe the old boomer rebels could understand and guide the next generation more than you think. Remember, before your generation "emerged" we were rebelling, and our revolution was successful!

DAVID: Yes, Woodstock and rock and roll and all that. But it didn't take long for the hippies to become yuppies, did it?

KEITH: Yes, the boomers started out as complainers, but they did something about what they didn't like, they turned their whining into working. Of course, I should remind you that the vast majority of boomers weren't really hippies. But let's use that broad brush to paint the entire generation. We saw what we didn't like, protested for a while, then took jobs and started making changes from the inside. They call that transition "hippies becoming yuppies," but it was really just a transition from whining to working to bring change. Instead of protesting from the outside, we came in and led an inside revolution in church structure and format. Of course, there were a ton of us, so we were hard to ignore.

DAVID: This issue of generational size is part of the rub. My generation is tiny in comparison, more like the "lost generation" born during the depression and through World War II. Many from my generation were aborted before birth; nearly a third of us were aborted.[1]

KEITH: That's a horrible thought.

DAVID: I have been wondering about these statistics the last few years. I'm not sure we've fully grasped the psychological effect of these deaths. Around 450,000 Americans died in World War II, and we have monuments and memorials all over our country to these soldiers. It was a defining moment for a generation. But much more than twice that figure die in America every year because of abortion.

I'm not sure we've registered how that affects the generations with missing brothers and sisters. There's something sad about our generation. We carry around a free-floating angst. Millions of us are missing. We are like surviving brothers and sisters of a family that discarded a third of its children. The mass media never talks about this, of course, so it's not in the public forum—it's a subconscious thing.

KEITH: This is a good thing to discuss because we mostly think of the affect of abortion on the parents. You've pointed out its effect on the younger generation. Good point. Even more, why not use that angst to change things in general?

DAVID: But most of my generation gave up before they started. They feel overlooked. All the attention goes to the boomer generation.

KEITH: That's how many of your generation often comes across to us.

DAVID: While they have not given up on making a difference locally, or trying something new in their local churches, many have almost given up hope as we carry around a free-floating grief. You boomers don't get it. And all this applies to leadership because we tend to dismiss leadership above the local level as something distant and unchanging and something we'll never have a chance to change. Many lay people in my generation simply let the boomers run the church boards and quietly ignore our own leadership responsibilities.

KEITH: I'm not sure your generation has given it a fair try. You will inherit the church no matter what. Time marches on.

DAVID: I hope we will be ready. There is a view among my generation that leadership is so out of touch and their methods and meetings are so antiquated, they seem irrelevant to us. Many of my generation simply ignore stuff from church leaders and do not aspire to leadership.

KEITH: One thing my generation was good at was using the methods of the previous generation to make changes. We got into the game and played ball, then took over and changed the ballgame. I've noticed that your generation often doesn't even show up at decision-making conferences, or when they do, they sit in the back, roll their eyes then leave early. These are the places where real change can be voted on, but many in your emerging generation blow off these meetings then grumble that nothing changes.

DAVID: That is true, I admit. Those meetings seem irrelevant to my generation. To us, few real changes seem to happen at them. It's depressing to us. The bigger problem lies in how to get into those venues. The people who make decisions are selected or voted into leadership and the younger generations are rarely on the list. The local church votes in their representatives, and they mostly send retired people or those already in the good-ol'-boy network. Then the district conferences forward these same folk to the general conference. The higher you go, the grayer your hair.

KEITH: You've named the problem for sure. The lay people from your generation will need to be willing to take a day off work to go to district conferences. The ministers in your age bracket already have a vote, but they'll have to use their votes and get behind one of their own. Your generation has to show up, speak up, and become candidates. However, don't think your generation alone expects change and can't get it. There are many with gray hair working for change and even worried that they have not been able to integrate the emerging generation into leadership. It is one of the major tasks of the coming decade for the boomers: coaching the emerging generation into leadership.

DAVID: That's a hopeful thought. I have heard many boomers say they want younger folk to participate. But are you ready for the way many of these younger leaders will lead?

KEITH: How's that?

DAVID: I see a marked trend among younger leaders to involve everyone they can in the decision-making process. They seem to be wary of authoritative Moses-on-the-mountain decision-making structures and reject from-behind-closed-doors pronouncements.

KEITH: Yes, I've seen that too. It's like your generation wants to take a poll and let everyone have their say before making any decision.

DAVID: When immature, it can seem like polling, but when it is intentional, the ownership resulting from that emerging kind of leadership is enormous. The younger leaders are comfortable in the ever-changing Facebook and Twitter-style open source environments where the playing field is flat and not hierarchical. To us, influence is earned through relationship and not through appointed positions. This has always been true to some extent, but it is particularly keen among younger generations.

KEITH: The seeds of that approach are long-standing in our heritage. Remember, Wesleyans were among the first denomination to expect every conference and board be made up of 50 percent laity and not stacked with a majority of ministers. It is true that in the last few decades we have opted for a more top-down approach, because that is what we were taught by our leadership gurus. We were taught to capture a vision on our own (or sometimes with a small group of insiders) then cast it to the members. But participation is still written on the books. We could elect a twenty-five-year old as a district superintendent or general superintendent if we wanted to—there are no written age restrictions.

DAVID: That doesn't sound much like the system we have today, however.

KEITH: True, but there are plenty of older folk who might delight in picking younger leaders if those younger leaders were willing and ready. There is plenty of power in the hands of the people in our denomination—if they take it.

DAVID: But younger folk in my generation don't know the ins and outs of the process. Many would rather just go off to plant a church or work on staff and just do our own thing. If the denomination doesn't bother us, we won't bother them.

KEITH: If you check out, you will be left out. Boomers will cling to their leadership slots way into their seventies and maybe eighties unless they see promising signs from the next generation. Leaders are notorious for saying, "I don't see anyone on the horizon, so I'll stay a bit longer." We boomers may define *leadership* differently than you do, but it is your generation's job to help us see your own approach as valid. Otherwise, we will dismiss you and leave you hiding, while we comfortably make our churches into senior citizen churches. But in our hearts, we don't want to become like those old downtown churches full of gray heads with no young people, so you have time on your side.

DAVID: So what should we do?

KEITH: Your generation has to quit standing on the sidelines and start getting involved in leading district and denominational work. You've got to make your case for a different kind of leadership. Help us understand that when you want to gather the people to ponder instead of making pronouncements, it is not a sign of weak leadership as we've taught each other. You need to show up, be positive, and play the game by the existing rules before taking charge and making new rules for the game. Your generation has to quit complaining that you don't get anything out of conferences or pastoral meetings. It will require switching your thinking from getting to giving—giving influence on what the district and denomination will become. Some from your generation are being elected to local church boards, and even to district and denominational boards and leadership positions. Get behind those and make sure they don't treat these responsibilities casually or make fun of their roles just to be popular with the sideliners. Boomers have no choice. We can't stay in control when we're ninety!

DAVID: This reminds us that it's a lot of work to change things. I do agree that we have a responsibility to engage and shouldn't expect the older generation to do the hard work of making the changes we want. It's our job. Attending some boring meetings might be the price to pay for greater influence. Volunteering to help some backward sounding project is a good step. I'm reminded of the quote: "you get the leaders you deserve." Maybe by standing on the sidelines, we are getting exactly what we deserve.

KEITH: Exactly. So what can my older generation do to help your generation assume greater leadership in the coming years?

DAVID: Senior pastors could take youth pastors aside and talk about broader leadership issues in a constructive way, coaching them on why it matters for them to be involved. An older conference veteran could drive to the conference with a younger delegate and discuss the ins and outs of what's happening and how to change things. I suspect that on a basic relational level there's a lot more in common than it seems.

KEITH: That's not too hard. Maybe the youth pastor can ask the senior pastor to ride along, instead of the youth pastor waiting for an invitation?

DAVID: Sure. But, I hear you talk about the boomers needing to learn to coach the next generation into leadership, but then you say things like that: "waiting for an invitation." It's like your generation views us as complaining brats instead of giving us some respect. I would ask for some openness to the views younger leaders have of these structures. Oftentimes their assessment is truthful; in fact, it's what your generation may want to say if you felt free to do so.

KEITH: OK, OK . . . I see what you're saying.

DAVID: And I'll concede that we do need to get involved for our part. I've heard your generation extolling the truth of the quote: "90 percent of success is showing up." So if that's true, then we've got the responsibility to do the most important thing—showing up. Just being there counts a lot.

KEITH: Especially when it comes time to vote. If the younger members of a church simply attended the local church conference, they could put one or two of their own generation on most local boards, even this year. It has to be someone both generations can support, but that can be figured out.

DAVID: OK, people in churches will be reading and discussing this chapter. Let's list some questions we've left unanswered here—things both generations in a local church ought to talk about concerning leadership in our denomination from the local church to the entire denomination.

Questions for Discussion

1. Of the North American adult population, about 35 percent are in their twenties and thirties. What percent of attendees of our local church are in their twenties and thirties? Are we getting our share, or are they missing?

2. How many members of our own local church are in their twenties and thirties?

3. What percent of our local church board are in their twenties and thirties?

4. What might be the reasons our church differs from the general population? Why do we have so many (or so few) of this generation attending? Leading?

5. What are the advantages to having people from the younger generation on the board in a local church? What are the risks or disadvantages?

6. What are the three biggest barriers that keep younger generations from entering leadership service in our own local church?

7. Who are some of the younger folk in our church who would make good leaders?

8. What signs do older generations look for in younger folk that make them feel confident they are prepared to take leadership?

9. What ways do the older generations in a local church sponsor or mentor younger generations into future leadership? Who are the good examples of this kind of mentoring in our church now? Who are the best candidates for this kind of mentoring in the future?

Notes

1. http://www.johnstonsarchive.net/policy/abortion/graphusabrate.html (accessed February 20, 2009). From the mid-70s to the mid-80s, the number of abortions compared to live-births was roughly 25–30 percent. For ten straight years, for every seven children born, three were aborted. And these numbers do not include miscarriages and fetal deaths. In 1975, there were more than a million abortions in the United States, and in no year since has the number been less than one million.

10

Ordained Ministry

What's the point of ordination, anyway? Isn't it just a piece of paper?

When that man fell from the ministry, it crushed my minister's spirit in many ways. It became hard to imagine taking up the same calling he had.

Why does our pastor insist on being called "Ron"? When I was growing up, we would have called him "Reverend Phillips" as a sign of respect.

I see a real trend these days of pastors going in and out of the ministry— like it's no longer a life-long calling. Isn't that a problem?

Half of these kids studying for the ministry will be working at places like Wal-Mart or Starbucks in six years. Is a ministry job "optional" for them?

Is ordination scriptural? I don't get it.

DAVID: In my training for the ministry, I had three key mentors—all of whom were ordained Wesleyan ministers—who were over me in leadership and who invested in me very intentionally. I looked up to them and wanted to be like them. Then in the span of eighteen months, two of them fell from the ministry. Both had inappropriate relationships outside of marriage and neither would submit at that time to a restoration process. They were not only secretly and carnally sinful (which happens); they were entirely rebellious and unwilling to submit to the community around them for reinstatement.

KEITH: Sin happens. I know those stories and grieve with you too.

DAVID: I praise the Lord that you were my third mentor, Dad. I think my heart was rescued from serious damage because I had another example. As this was all going down publicly, I saw many friends in ministry slide one of two directions: (1) right out of full time ministry in the church; or (2) into a cynical, distrustful, depressing view of leadership. I had an advantage over them, which several have directly pointed out to me, so I can't imagine the full extent of the pain they feel.

KEITH: Yes, it's depressing when ministers fall, especially our famous heroes. I have my own list too, and it includes people like college presidents who lied and were removed, district superintendents who went to jail because of sexual involvement with minors, and pastors and college professors who were tangled up in sin. These tragedies are not new. My father had his own list too, though I never knew about it as a young person. They kept these things quieter then. As an old man, he told me the stories of old fashioned, holiness preachers who had fallen. His list was just as long as mine. Sin sometimes happens. Ministers fall from grace. Great heroic leaders fall too, maybe more so. I don't know if it is more common today than ever, but it is more public. Perhaps it is worse because we elevate great leaders more today, and our hero worship is more easily disappointed, so we are more inclined to become disillusioned.

DAVID: Those are good words for my friends, some of whom still can't get back on track toward ministry due to the crushing disappointment from their hero's fall. But fallen leaders are just part of a larger issue; the erosion of trust in ministers and leaders among the younger generations is great. Sometimes it has been the sexual sins of leaders. However, as you've told me, there are two common ways to fall from the ministry: the fast way and the slow way. The fast way is sexual indiscretion; the slow way is financial indiscretion. Whether fast or slow, both are dangerous. Just this past week, a Wesleyan church and its Christian school hit the papers publicly because the financial manager (who supervised the finances of both) was charged with embezzling over 250,000 dollars. I worry about the few hundred kids in that school and church that have just had another huge chunk of trust eroded. What's more, there are those in the community who really didn't need yet another reason to distrust the leadership of Christians.

KEITH: Yes, sex and money are two common exits from the ministry. However, today another common exit (even more then money) is disillusionment or burnout. This brings us back to the above discussion. It could be that disillusionment is just as dangerous as adultery or embezzlement when it comes to destroying the ministerial callings of young men and women. But, where are you going with all this, David? Yes, we can only give our full trust to God and not to human leaders, but what's the larger concern?

DAVID: Ordained ministry and authority in general is the larger concern. So much of this sin and positional abuse can be traced to lack of accountable leaders, those who have been set apart and set over the people in authority, because of a piece of paper called ordination. It seems like the church drastically needs to reevaluate whether so sharp a distinction between lay and ordained people is as useful as it once was. Of course, it has been a problem in all traditions. These days the Roman Catholic Church is in major crisis in many regions as priests have been prosecuted as predatory pedophiles, abusing their power over the young.

KEITH: The Roman Catholic system of male-only celibate priests is somewhat different, and the rigid power system has sometimes protected sinning priests. The Wesleyan system is not perfect, but we are less likely to protect and cover up sin in the ministry.

DAVID: True, we haven't been hit with anything so widespread, but I suspect our elevation of the ordained minister is susceptible to similar problems. Some in my generation think we ought to do away with professional ministerial class. We wonder if we have made an unnecessary distinction by elevating ministers above the people when in fact they are no better than the average layperson.

KEITH: As Wesleyans, we can do anything we want. We don't place our ministers on as high a pedestal as Roman Catholic priests, and we don't grant them as much authority as an Episcopal system would, but we do set aside some of our ordinary Christians as elders or ministers just like the apostle Paul did.

DAVID: I really enjoyed your book *Call of a Lifetime*. I've even used it as a textbook in facilitating ministerial training. But in one section of that book, you elevate the ordained ministry to a near priestly function.

KEITH: That is technically how we see it. When ordained ministers lay hands on a ministerial candidate, we are reflecting the idea that an unbroken chain of ordained ministers have laid hands on successive generations of ministers all the way back to the apostles. But in practice, we don't act like this. While ministers (especially in larger churches) might take huge authority as a CEO, they are less likely to take priestly or prophetic authority in practice. But, yes, technically Wesleyans do set apart ministers as representing God to the people and the people to God.

DAVID: That's where my generation challenges your description of ministry. I've seen others bristle at that idea too. How can you say that an ordained minister "represents God to the people and the people to God"? Perhaps my view on this is still stuck in the reformation debates, but it's hard for me to imagine bailing on the idea of there being no mediator between God and man but Christ. Have you edited that protest out of the Protestant Reformation?

KEITH: Look at it this way: When a minister preaches a sermon, whom are they representing—themselves or God? Preaching is just that: representing God to the people—speaking words that God has laid on the heart of the pastor for the people.

When ministers pray the pastoral prayer, what are they doing—speaking to the people or to God? They are representing the people to God—speaking on behalf of the people and to God.

That's what a minister does. Like Moses, we do our best to speak to God on behalf of the people, and we speak to the people on behalf of God. Jesus Christ is the only mediator for our salvation, but that does not exclude others speaking for God or interceding for the people with God.

DAVID: Speaking to God for the people is a bit easier to swallow than speaking to the people for God. Yes, we may need an appointed spokesperson for the act of confession and intercession in prayer. But when you describe the preaching act as "speaking for God," we get a bit nervous. There is just so much abuse that can take place when a minister has that attitude about their words, and even more when a whole church sees the preacher that way. That's when a group starts to get pretty close to drinking the Kool-Aid, if you catch my drift.

KEITH: Anything powerful is prone to abuse. That doesn't disqualify the power; it just proves how powerful it is. There is a true power in preaching that can be and, sadly, is sometimes abused by ministers, but that doesn't mean God doesn't want people to speak for him. The Bible is a long record of people speaking for God. But, I do see your generation's concern. In fact, seldom can I urge my students in homiletics to say much with certainty. They say "in my opinion" or "I personally think" and are very reluctant to say anything with certainty representing God.

DAVID: To us, the message from a pastor is not on par with the Bible. Scripture speaks for God; preachers interpret and apply it.

KEITH: Yes, I agree. But, in interpretation and application, they try their best to speak for God in this present situation.

DAVID: In that process, we can get off track. You describe the Moses-like quality of a preacher going up the mountain to get the message and proclaim it. That process is so often faked, that a more authentic approach might be to live in and among the people. We can keep the message edit-able and then speak to the people—from the people. Even great preachers like Steve DeNeff, (whom I work for) keep this tension alive. Staff and other advisors discuss and debate his message ideas before they are given; then afterwards, people discuss and apply it in classes and groups. The message is a living thing, not a moment in time where the perfect thing was said and never questioned.

KEITH: Sure, but even in those discussions (which I take part in every week), there is a larger submission to the words spoken from the pulpit. There's a sense that the message is given the benefit of the doubt, it is the trump card, all else being equal. The message from Scripture is where we hear from God, even though some of the thoughts are the preacher's, and we can take or leave that part.

DAVID: Perhaps our differences here point to a broader change in emphasis beyond just preaching. A lot of us emerging young leaders today are advocating for an equality of leadership. First, there is a de-emphasis on ordination as the ticket to certain ministry tasks. Preaching, visiting hospitals, baptizing people—these are all held much looser among the young. We want to raise up the church to engage in all the tasks of the church, truly being a priesthood of all believers.

KEITH: Sure, that's OK with my generation. In the '60s, we led that revolution. We are the ones who quit putting clergy stickers on our cars and quit asking for clergy discounts at stores, and we are the ones who exchanged the title "Reverend Drury" for "Pastor Keith." We are the generation who quit wearing ties to the church office and told people they were just as called to ministry as a pastor. In fact, this was Jim Garlow's specialty for many years. You might be reacting to the more recent spate of CEO-ism that came with the '80s church growth movement. It is true that many pastors became CEOs during the '80s and expected the people to become followers.

DAVID: We can only respond to the church we experienced, not the one that went before in history. So we know little of the pre-CEO pastor you're talking about. The second thing you'll see among the young is an attempt to re-language the ordained role. You already see *Reverend* used seldom. Many pastors are no longer even called "Pastor Keith" in their churches. Keith just happens to be the lead pastor or teaching pastor in the church and doesn't want to be put on a pedestal by the people.

KEITH: These changes only continue the trajectory already in place. I see little challenge from the boomers here, other than CEO-pastors scoffing at your asking the people or thinking everyone has to put in their two cents worth before making a decision.

As I've mentioned, The Wesleyan Methodist Church was the first denomination in America to insist that all denominational and college committees and boards be made up of 50 percent laity. In fact, the founding leaders resisted centralized power and authority so much that they would not even call themselves a denomination. They named themselves the Wesleyan Methodist Connection. The idea of a bishop would have made them tremble in fear or anger. If you younger folk democratize all discussions and decision-making, you will be squarely in the center of our early history, even though it will look like a revolution to the more recent pastor-as-CEO-ism.

DAVID: OK, well, I guess many of these changes are more of a reaction to the recent history of church growth than the long-held tradition. A third way things will change as my generation takes over relates to the call. Many younger pastors consider everyone to be called to careers and paths of leadership in the kingdom of God, not just ministers. What's more, many younger pastors are OK with leaving the active ministry in a church job to serve in non-pastoral ministry for a while and re-enter church pastoral work later on. The transition line between the ordained ministry and general ministry is less rigid for many of my generation. We see all Christians as called.

KEITH: This is an interesting shift; I see it among the young people I teach and in the institution where I work which has a "Life-Calling center" for all students. My students are inclined to think of the call to ministry as a leading that is no different from the calling to be a nurse or teacher.

For most of Christian church history, we have considered the call to ministry as a lifetime matter, something more like marriage. We admit that sometimes people leave the ministry, and sometimes ministers fall from grace and have to be removed, but we have tended toward the two thousand-year history of considering "the call" a lifetime thing.

Our denomination provides for a less-than-lifetime church work by allowing for lay positions—full time, non-ordained staff positions. A person can lead the youth or be a staff person in all kinds of other ministries as a layperson without committing to a life of ordained ministry. If they want to do ministry for a decade then open up a coffee shop, there is no shame. However, Wesleyans have stuck with the long catholic history of considering ordained ministry a lifetime commitment and commission.

Before your generation tampers too much with that model, you'll want to do some serious thinking. Maybe you'll invent new categories of ministry for those in your generation who want to do church work for a while then move on to other things. And for sure, you need to investigate the life calling that every person can have. These things have all been investigated in the past and can be revisited. After all, it is your church too, and what we have now is not set in stone.

DAVID: These are all good responses, for sure. I suppose you did write the book on it.

KEITH: True, I did write a book on it. That book reflected what we believe and practice now, but new books will be written later reflecting new approaches to ministry. Maybe your generation will dig up Jim Garlow's writing or start writing books yourselves. When you do, you will have to hammer out your own approach to the call to ministry and the general life calling of all Christians. Maybe you'll improve on what our generation wrote and practiced. If you carefully consider the thousands-year-old tradition of the church and come up with something better, great!

Eventually your generation will have to move beyond questioning what you received to putting forth your own comprehensive approach and letting others judge the plan. Maybe you'll ordain every single Christian in the future. Who knows?! Maybe you'll do away completely with all paid staff at churches and everything will be lay-led and all ministers will become bi-vocational. Maybe you'll rotate eldership among the laity in the future. Whatever you do, it will have to be thoughtful and comprehensive and accepted by the whole church. Then you will have to defend it when the next generation comes along asking these kinds of questions of your model.

DAVID: You are fair in criticizing our generation for seeing problems with the present system without suggesting a complete new model. Some of my generation have been thinking about this; eventually some of us will go to press. One thing that is very distasteful to us is when ministers lord it over the church. We expect ministers to be one of the people—not elevated so high they are somehow too special.

KEITH: That's fair. Every Wesleyan minister is instructed to avoid "lording it over the flock" when we are ordained. Some obey this instruction; some don't. You and I have no quarrel here.

I do admit that since the 1970s, there has been a strong Wesleyan movement toward investing greater power in the clergy and denominational leaders. I believe it is no accident that this occurred simultaneously with the increased number of mega-churches. We boomers tend to see church-work as a sprawling, massive, complex enterprise requiring specialization and strong leadership from professionals—more like a business than the church we grew up with. We remember smaller churches where the laity controlled everything and ministers were treated as employees. Maybe we have gone too far now. Maybe there needs to be a new movement the other way.

If God calls younger folk to lead this movement to raise the commitment and involve the laity, then do it! After all, in the not-too-distant future, many of us boomer ministers will be retiring, and we will be attending *your* churches. As retired ministers in your churches, we might like a stronger say in things!

DAVID: Oh boy, let's not even get into that. What I do think is that we have laid out the generational issues here of clergy and laity. And we have opened up the matter of the call, lifetime or otherwise. Let's write some questions to focus the ongoing conversation in local churches.

Questions for Discussion

1. How do you remember ministers being treated in the past compared to today? What have been good changes and what do you think have been bad changes?

2. Do you feel called to your profession (speaking here to those who are not ordained ministers)? If so, how is your call different or similar to a minister's call?

3. What are the advantages of having a fifty-fifty representation of laity and ministers on all boards and committees above the local church in a denomination? Disadvantages? What other kinds of representation could we consider?

4. To what extent is the leveling value of many younger folk a good or bad value? What do you think of the trend of the last thirty years of centralization and increased authority for pastors and denominational leaders? What do you think the future holds: more of the same or a reversal of this trend?

5. Is there a way to raise the importance of lay life calling without reducing the importance of a ministerial calling? Or, should the ministerial calling be emphasized less in the future? In recent years, how has the status or power of a minister increased or decreased?

6. Who was called to ministry in the Bible? Were there people who entered the priesthood or ministry for a while, then left it later? Do you consider Luke a layman or a minister? What about the apostles? Phoebe? Barnabas? Priscilla?

7. What exactly are we doing when we ordain a minister? Why do we ordain ministers? Why don't we ordain laity? Is the calling of a minister irrevocable and for a whole lifetime, or is it OK for a minister to leave ministry and start an insurance agency at the age of fifty? When ministers retire, are they leaving the ministry? When a woman minister leaves the pastorate to raise her children for two decades, is that OK or does she have to stay in pastoral work continually to be ordained?

8. What are the categories of non-ordained ministry in our denomination and how often do we use them? Should there be more categories? Does anyone in this group remember what lay preachers were?

9. How does our church's size affect our view of the professional ministry? Lay leadership?

10. If you were designing the denomination on blank paper, how would you design ordination, the ministry, and the laity?

11

Intergenerational Dialogue

DAVID: We've hit on several of the primary issues our two generations need to talk about, but the list could go on and on. There are plenty of other points of debate and differences between the generations, and there's a lot of change in the air.

KEITH: You bet. We haven't even touched on politics, ecclesiology, broader social justice issues, or even Christology and its exclusiveness— all areas where emerging generations seem to have some differences with us older folk.

DAVID: And I imagine there will be new issues coming up in the next few years. Medical ethics, the Internet church, and reverse missions all seem to be right around the corner to discuss and find our way in the church, all generations together.

KEITH: Well, we can't cover everything in one book and even if we did, there would be new issues that emerged as soon as the book was printed. This has been a good place to start in opening a dialogue between generations. This has been helpful for me.

DAVID: I'm thankful you've been willing to bat around these ideas. I know many of these things make your generation uncomfortable. It has been helpful to hear your unfiltered responses and to hear how you and other older generations might feel about them. I've learned a lot.

KEITH: Thanks for listening and for being open to hear my perspective. Perhaps the biggest reason for this book is there's not enough inter-generational dialogue on issues like these. The generations may not be listening to each other.

DAVID: Or they haven't found a forum where listening could happen. That's why I'm excited about the possibility of people from several generations discussing this book together. A discussion like that could open up the dialogue on what we want to become in the future. Also, it would help my generation keep the baby while tossing out the bath-water.

KEITH: So, what have we learned in our intergenerational dialogue here that could be passed on?

DAVID: One of the key learning points for me is that while I often assume the older generation's reactions to change are based on philosophical issues, it's often more spiritual and emotional at the core. As a pastor, I think I've underestimated how talking about change in worship, or how people are converted, or how we see heaven can actually hurt someone. It's scary to me to think my generation's leadership could actually cause harm to people spiritually.

KEITH: I'm glad you've picked up on that. Older folk are just as worthy of being cared for as younger and unchurched folk. For me, a key learning point is that we can't pigeonhole what we think younger generations believe. I've often heard things younger leaders say and interpreted them as threatening and dangerous ideas, when in reality some of these ideas are merely a return to something my parents might have espoused (and my generation tossed out as bathwater). Your generation sure gets there differently, but some of the ideas I'm hearing from you and others are more of a rediscovery of something old rather than initiating something new.

DAVID: I think that about your generation too. I often think of the boomers as being so traditional, when in reality, the reactions I am hearing are often a defense of the revolutionary changes you have already made. It seems like your generation feels like they made a lot of progress in the last thirty years and hate to see it undone by changes we want to make.

KEITH: That hits the nail on the head. We do feel that way at times. Nobody is as conservative as former revolutionaries now in power.

DAVID: Knowing that helps me understand that your generation's intent is not just to keep it like you've always done it, but often is to preserve changes you really thought through in the past. That is why you tried a new way. Of course, that does not mean you always did it right. At least you were trying!

KEITH: Another thing I learned in this discussion is how much the younger generation wants mentoring and sponsoring. Boomers pretty much wanted to be left alone by the older generations. You guys want to be mentored, guided, and sponsored by us. When we leave you alone, it is not a gift but a curse to you.

DAVID: Yes, we yearn for relationships with older generations, not just people our own age. One of the things that has been so helpful in this dialogue is when you've given a bit of advice on how to lead the older generations. Your tips have helped me know the way to approach the subject in the future, while also giving me a sense of responsibility, as a pastor, not to try to win the argument, but to shepherd people through these concerns.

KEITH: Yes. Win the hearts of the people, not just their heads. Another thing I learned is the necessity of a formal process of dialogue for this kind of open discussion. We've batted around some of these ideas while hiking together or on Christmas vacations, but writing this book together enabled both of us to articulate our differences and shared values far better than in our random conversations.

DAVID: Exactly. This is why people from both generations, both laity and church staffs, need to use this book in some formal way to open up a dialogue together. When there is a scheduled time to talk and a specific agenda of the issues, I think the generations in the church can find greater unity and common purpose. I hope people aren't content with only reading this on their own without doing what we've done in this book—talking together.

KEITH: You bet. Perhaps some Sunday school classes and small groups will use the chapters to open these discussions. Even where the generations represent different positions than we took here, what we really need is an open and honest discussion about what we will become in the future. If we do not talk about it together, we will drift along with the world and evangelical culture never knowing who we are and where we are going. In larger churches, where there are several generations serving on the church staff, they could schedule a regular talk time to hash out some of these things.

DAVID: Exactly. I guess we're both saying that the value of this book might be less about the content we wrote than the model—talking together honestly, sharing our perspectives, and trying to come together. What we need is a lot of discussion about the future of the church in every corner of the kingdom. Some of that discussion will be about practical issues, like how to elect pastors or our denominational leaders; but it must also deal with the major issues that are shaping our denomination today without our knowing it. The future of every denomination is in our hands together, and we need to do something with it, not leaving it to the influence of people outside the denomination. I hope my generation can introduce change without the kind of conflict that your generation's worship wars brought in the past. We'd rather talk it out together like we've done here than just slam changes down the older people's throats.

KEITH: Sure, I think the boomers will talk, as you said earlier, if you schedule it. So, what are some practical things you would say to your own generation about entering into a generational dialogue on these or other issues that might come up?

DAVID: For those youth pastors out there who think their senior pastor is out of touch on so many things, I would encourage them to get creative in finding ways to talk about things together. Boomers may be more open to new ideas than they think. I'd suggest scheduling a once a month lunch or breakfast meeting with their older senior pastor just to talk about ministry philosophies. I think they'll get more traction in their work and maybe these younger pastors will learn a lot too, if they keep an open mind. Boomers like to talk about how they changed things (for instance, you just went on and on about it for most of this book!). If we can get the boomers talking, they will reflect more on what changes were not so perfect after all.

KEITH: I think that would work. Older generations need to feel like they are investing in those conversations rather than just arguing. Boomers feel like they've won all the arguments with the generation before them, so they don't like being placed in the older generation category yet. While boomers are still are in charge, they will respond best when asked questions, asked for advice, and asked how they accomplished change in the past. Boomers are better at answering and telling than asking and pondering.

DAVID: I really hope this book prompts two classes of different ages to merge for a while to talk about these issues. The worship arts director in my church did several separate generational conversations where people could talk frankly, then brought them all together to look at the results and had some more good dialogue. Our church has five generations very strongly represented (which is rare for many churches today), and it was enlightening to see the views of each written down in black and white on response sheets that we looked at together. How about you? What are some practical things you'd suggest the older generations do in order to achieve some helpful dialogue.

KEITH: We've mentioned generations of ministers talking together and Sunday school classes and small groups of lay people dialoging, but how about district minister's retreats where there are several generations? How about denominational think tanks? If we gather denominational thinkers together and spend too much time on structure and election processes, while ignoring some of these massive generational shifts taking place under the water, we will have frittered away our time.

How about families? Could families discuss these issues on Christmas break as we have done? I also suspect there could be some excellent open and respectable discussion on blogs and social networking sites. I am encouraged to see how many of my generation are present and discussing things there. These issues in reality ought to be hammered out in that virtual reality too.

DAVID: Great additions! Why don't we close out this book and prompt the conversation with a few questions to get that kind of discussion going? If a person is reading this book by him- or herself, what are the questions they might ask to get their own discussion going—questions that might lead to something more formal and scheduled, like a class or discussion group?

Questions to Think about After Reading This Book Alone

1. Who from another generation could I loan this book to in order to see if they'd be interested in sponsoring an intergenerational discussion group with me on the future of our church?

2. If people from several generations got together in my church to discuss these issues, who are some of the key people who ought to be in that conversation?

3. Which two Sunday school classes or small groups now represent differing generations could be combined for a time to talk about these things?

4. What class or group could invite members of another generation into its existing class for a period of discussion about these things?

5. Who might make a good moderator or facilitator of an open discussion between the generations in our church—someone who didn't have to talk a lot, but could moderate a discussion?

Questions to Discuss After Reading This Book with Other Generations

1. What are the top five issues (in this book or beyond it) that the generations in your church still need to talk more about?

2. What is the elephant-in-the-room issue in your church where the generations are still far apart? How can this conversation go on in order to carve out the future?

3. Who are some of the good examples of people in your church that are great models of intergenerational listening and discussion? Who should we all try to be more like when talking with other generations?

4. What kind of periodic format could be introduced where the generations come together for continuing discussions from time to time? Who would initiate that? How often? Where?

5. What person in another generation have you come to appreciate and admire more through these intergenerational discussions? What specifically do you appreciate about them?

Teacher Tips

To facilitate intergenerational dialogue, use these tips and the questions at the end of each chapter for leading class and group discussions of this book.

1
Worship

1. What songs have the deepest meaning to you personally? Why?

   Have participants list several songs, writing them on the board. Try to determine together why these songs are so meaningful.

2. If you were facing a slow death with cancer, what songs would come to your mind as fortifying to your faith during a time of difficulty?

   You could list these songs on the board too. Look for the "flavor" of each generation's musical preferences.

3. What songs from the past or present feel shallow to you? Why?

   You will probably find some shallowness in all generational music and, in the process, find why some songs offer deeper meaning.

4. What is missing in the music at your worship service that you wish could be added?

   Avoid an ain't-it-awful tone by aiming this discussion at what songs should be added and how they might be added in the future—even during this group meeting. Perhaps sing some of these songs together.

5. What positive or negative symbolism does bright or dim lighting in worship communicate to you personally?

   Help both generations see this symbolism as being determined by their own experiences. Help both generations see these methods as a moving target. Aim for understanding.

6. What do you think of worship venues where the musical style is targeted to one style preference?

   Be honest—note the problems with this method, but also list some values.

7. What are the advantages and disadvantages to blended worship in a single worship service?

   List both advantages and disadvantages together, aiming to find that no method works for everyone, and we all must have some flexibility in a loving community.

8. How can worship leaders of any age get feedback from the worshipers so they are helping all to worship the best they can?

   Brainstorm ways for worship leaders to get feedback. Maybe even invite your worship leader to the group meeting for this discussion, or produce some suggestions for your worship leader. If you are the worship leader, collect ideas and implement at least one feedback system.

9. What are the wrong and right things to do when worship music does not satisfy us?

   This will be easy—have fun listing the "how not to" responses first, followed by the "how to" responses.

10. How can people of all ages learn to be more pliable and accepting of the various languages of worship music?

   This is the crux of the discussion. Work together as a group to create a list of attitudes and approaches that everyone can embrace.

11. Are there any older hymns that you wish younger people would learn the lyrics to?

   Let the older generation list them; maybe even sing some together.

12. Are there any new songs that you wish older people would learn the lyrics to?

   Perhaps this will come from the younger generations, but let everyone list songs they'd like to hear more often. Make sure your worship leader receives a copy of the list; if you only make the list and do nothing with it, this will be a useless exercise. Wind up the group by having participants share what they've learned from the discussion that brought them greater understanding of other views.

Conversion

1. What are the strengths of the ticket-to-heaven or decision approach to evangelism? What are the weaknesses?

   As a group, list the strengths of this method of evangelism. (Wait until later to discuss its weaknesses.) As you move through the first three questions, try to guide the group away from enshrining any one approach as the only way to do evangelism.

2. What were the strengths of the revival altar call approach to evangelism? Weaknesses?

   Again, list only the strengths at this point. Invite stories, if anyone would like to share.

3. What are the strengths of the journey approach to evangelism? Weaknesses?

   Since fewer people may be familiar with this approach, you may have to imagine together what advocates of the journey approach might say about its strengths and list them on the board. Be as fair and charitable as possible. Then, work your way through all three approaches again, this time discussing the weaknesses of each.

4. Search for and make a list of the ways people were converted in Scripture. What similarities are there? What differences?

   Have the group think of at least six conversion stories from the Bible and identify which method was used in each. How was the apostle Paul converted? Luke? The Philippian jailer? The woman at the well? The thousand at Pentecost? You will probably find a variety of ways. Discuss the similarities and differences.

5. What do you think of churches numerically reporting conversions at the end of a church year? How do we know a person is converted?

   Lead a serious discussion on when we can count conversions and even if we should count them. Avoid divisiveness and lead the discussion toward intergenerational understanding.

6. Are more people getting saved gradually today than in the past? How does a person get saved gradually? What kind of cross-the-line moments should a church offer for people?

   Invite testimonies at this point. Do you have anyone in the group who was saved gradually? Guide the discussion toward the importance of a crossing-the-line moment—perhaps baptism or a public testimony.

7. The oldest folk in a church and the younger ones often like personal testimonies or narrative approaches. Why do many in between not like this approach? What are the dangers of authentic testimonies?

   This is a good time to invite stories of the abuses of testimonies in the past; also list some of the strengths of this approach—work for cross-generational understanding.

8. What are some ideas for the future for helping people become truly converted and not just getting their ticket punched?

   Make a list as a group. All generations want true conversion, not just an assent or a nod. Guide the discussion toward ideas to enable full and true conversion.

9. Considering evangelism in our own church, what should be left as it is? What should we change?

   List both options on the board—"leave it be" and "change it"—then invite the group to fill in both columns. Urge the group to come together and agree on a few items.

10. How can the church do better at making disciples, not just making converts?

    Brainstorm ideas verbally, and then ask the group to come up with a list of the group's five best ideas for making better disciples. Wind up the group by having participants share what they've learned today that brought them greater understanding of other views.

3

Community

1. Describe the kind of community you experienced in the church where you were raised. If you were unchurched, where did you find community?

   Use this time to invite stories—have at least five people share their story. The discussion should bring a hunger for greater community.

2. Tell about the most significant community you experienced in this church in the last few years. What made this experience stand out for you?

   Gather stories. Let the idea of community become pervasive, inducing hunger for greater community. This discussion will show that your own church does have ways of experiencing community and you will likely discover the keys to community creation.

3. If people started attending this church on Sunday mornings and wanted to break into friendship, what would they need to do beyond attending a service? How would they know this?

   Use this discussion to clarify why some never find community in your church—they do not know or take the steps to find it. Discuss how to clarify the route to community in your church to those hungering for it.

4. About what size group is ideal for developing close community? How big does a group have to get before it is too large for creating intimate friendships?

   You may discover that breaking into smaller units (like your class or group) is the primary way. But you may also find dinners together, working together, and serving together in smaller groups are key.

5. What role does family play in community? If people have lots of relatives nearby, how does it help or hinder making new friendships?

   Lead a frank discussion of how family can help or hinder the development of community for those with no family in the church.

6. What groups does our church already have that provide community for those in them?

   Make a list together.

7. About how many people do you think you can have a deep friendship with?

   Invite sharing and discussion. Different people will give different numbers. Some folk will list a small number—maybe even two or three; others will list as many as forty. There is no right answer here, but it will clarify for the group how people relate. Discuss how a married couple sometimes has a different number and how this factors into their friendships.

8. Who are your deepest friends in life now—those you share most openly with? How many are in this church?

   This discussion can be affirming when people name names. It also leads your group to discover how many close friends may be outside of the church. Discuss what sort of balance is best.

9. What might we do in our church's regularly scheduled services and programming to promote the development of greater *koinonia*?

   Collect ideas and pass them on to the proper person.

10. In what sort of setting here at our church do people over age sixty-five experience community? Singles under thirty? Those with small children? Those who are middle-aged or empty nesters?

    In a verbal discussion, list these. If you find a gap, think of new ways to offer community for the missing link. See if someone in the group will take steps to fill the gap.

11. What new groups could be formed in our church to provide greater friendships and intimacy among our people? Who might be the likely person to start them?

Lead the brainstorming toward action—see if someone in your group will take action to start something.

12. In what way has this group—the group studying this book—become friends and developed deeper connection?

Lead an affirming time of sharing how community has grown in this group and why. Wind up the group by having participants share what they've learned today that brought them greater understanding of other views.

4

Race

1. Were you around during the civil rights years? What do you remember about the debates and the context back then? Did you speak up then?

   Avoid politicizing this discussion; keep the discussion to the church instead of wandering into politics or what is merely politically correct. Help younger generations learn from older generations who lived during this volatile time.

2. What lingering problems related to race are there in your community?

   Lead an open and honest sharing of stories from your own town.

3. What should the role of your church be when it comes to racial tensions in a community?

   Again, avoid a polarizing political discussion and keep the discussion to the role of the church and Christians.

4. What is the largest racial minority in your community?

Most will know this, but if you want to show the facts, consider assigning someone to look up local demographic data at your census bureau site online. Often there are hidden ethnic communities in a town that few know about. If you use research, turn the data into numbers of people—not just percentages. The church works with people, not percentages.

5. What could we do in the future as a denomination to ensure we are dealing with race in a way that honors God?

Keep the discussion positive—how our denomination can honor God through future actions.

6. How would we know when we've gone too far in this discussion about race? Is there a risk of being too politically correct here?

Without abandoning God's values, be frank about listing some cautions; yet urge the group to not blow off God's values by labeling righteous actions as mere political correctness. Invite all generations to speak honestly but always under God and not as a political statement.

7. Have you ever been to a racial reconciliation service? What was good and bad about that experience?

If people have attended one of these services, let them tell their story. If not, look at the Scripture's teaching on what we are to do when a brother or sister has something against us.

8. If you or your group were assigned the task to design a race confession service like the one discussed in this chapter, what elements would you include that would be meaningful? (Write this plan on a separate sheet of paper.)

   Brainstorm what a gathering of Christians might actually do. Think about the dangers and advantages of such a service. Think of other lower-risk ways of doing this. Imagine how such a service would work even between two groups of same-race people who are divided. Discuss how a service like this could become merely window-dressing too.

9. What are the issues today that young adults are being silent on that our children might ask us if we were present or absent?

   It is easy for younger generations to judge older folk on race. Turn the attention in this question to social issues today where younger people may be silent and might be judged by their own children later. Close the group by having participants share what they've learned today that brought them greater understanding of other views.

5
Heaven

1. Do you think heaven has been over-emphasized or under-emphasized.

   Your discussion may reveal differences among your group. Guide the discussion to understanding between generations. Discuss why younger folk sometimes seem to dismiss heaven and the afterlife.

2. What do you think heaven and the resurrection will be like?

   This is a fun discussion and it may be mostly imagination. Have several people share how they imagine heaven and what the resurrection will be like.

3. As a group, make a list of Scriptures that speak of the afterlife. What do these teach?

   You could assign someone ahead of time to bring Scriptures. Otherwise, use some of the common Scriptures on heaven such as: Psalm 2:4; 16:11; 17:15; 103:20, 22; Isaiah 33:17; Matthew 5:20; 22:30; 25:34; Luke 22:30; 23:43; 2 Corinthians 12:2, 4; Galatians 5:21; 2 Thessalonians 1:7; Revelation 5:9; 7:16–17; 12:7–9; 21:4, 22–27; 22:1–5.

4. How do these Scriptures motivate you to change things now?

Discuss heaven as a motivational force. You may find difference in approaches here—seek cross-generational understanding in the discussion. Invite older folk to share how they saw heaven as a young person.

5. How do these Scriptures reassure you about the future?

This is an excellent time to let older folk testify about the afterlife's role in their walk.

6. If our bodies are resurrected like orthodox Christian theology says, what do you think our bodies will be like in the afterlife?

This is mostly conjecture, but we have some evidence—Jesus Christ was resurrected and appeared for forty days. What was his body like?

7. Do you think there will be animals—even pets—in heaven? Defend your answer one way or the other.

This may seem to be pure fantasy, but there is a deeper theological discussion you might find here: How much does God restore—only humans or does he restore all of creation?

8. How can funerals avoid merely celebrating a person's life on earth, but also look forward to the resurrection and the after-life?

Guide the discussion on how Christians should face death differently than atheists. The discussion here is not useless conjecture but provides a basis for facing death and dying.

9. As a group, pretend you are a funeral planning committee. What would make a funeral more Christian?

Lead a practical discussion of how we can make Christian funerals more Christian. Close the group by having participants share what they've learned today that brought them greater understanding of other views.

6

Alcohol

1. What changes have you seen in church membership commitments during your lifetime?

   This chapter could produce a volatile discussion, so be careful in your group to keep things calm and loving. Start by looking back, with the older folk telling how some things have changed since their own youthful days. Use the discussion as a teaching time from older generations to younger ones. It starts mostly with older folk remembering the changes from the past—not the most recent changes, but those since their youthful days.

2. How did these things change?

   Have older folk describe how some of the rules in their church changed—the process that loosened or tightened some of the rules they lived under as youth. Help younger generations see several things that have changed over time and how.

3. What were some of the good changes in your opinion? Bad changes?

   Invite older folk to share here—telling their own story in an effort to bring understanding.

4. What were some of the expectations years ago that weren't even written down but were still expected of all serious church members?

These are different from written rules. Have older folk share some of the expectations they submitted to (or rebelled against) that weren't written down. Tell stories for the benefit of younger folk.

5. What is the purpose of membership commitments?

Before even discussing alcohol, ask this important question. Why have a list of commitments for church members? Try to list together the reason for these no matter what the issue.

6. What is the purpose of membership itself? What do you think of the no-membership idea?

Go even further upstream by discussing why we have membership at all.

7. Where would you draw the line on refusing to accept a new member?

Have several people share their thoughts. There will be differences here; keep those differences from causing division between people. Ask, "In your opinion, what would it take to refuse a new person membership?"

8. What would it take to get a member expelled from your church? Has it ever happened? How?

See if these standards differ from the above list. Ask why. Discuss how one corrects a member and who should do it.

9. If your group were making membership commitments for the entire denomination on blank paper, what would you require?

If your group were empowered to make the membership commitments for the entire denomination on blank paper, see what you would all agree on.

10. Do you think a full member should be able to drink a glass of wine with a meal? If so, how many? Scripture condemns drunkenness—how would drinkers know they have crossed this line? How is your position rooted in the Bible's teaching?

Here we come to the subject of this chapter and—properly so— after a broader discussion. Ask these questions in a thoughtful way and guide the discussion as if you were really creating the statement. Turn the discussion toward the Bible's role in designing membership commitments (as a transition to the next question).

11. Do you think that all membership commitments should be directly tied to Scripture? If so, what is your view on pornography or legal marijuana use (as it is in some states and countries)? What other things do you think are wrong, yet there is no specific verse about them in the Bible?

   Guide the discussion on this touchy subject. For most denominations, the Bible is their basis. Yet we have used Bible principles and values to oppose things that are not specifically addressed in the Bible—like slavery and alcohol. Get the group to list other things which the Bible does not condemn explicitly by name yet we have come to believe they are wrong. There will be differences here—but guide the discussion so that greater understanding of the other view results.

12. Does a denomination have a right to make membership requirements? Why or why not?

   Make two lists—why denominations do or don't have the right to make rules or expect promises of members. Seek consensus. Close the group by having participants share what they've learned today that brought them greater understanding of other views.

7

Sanctification

1. What were the seven vertical approaches to holiness that various denominations embrace to answer the question, "How saved can you be?" See if you can list them and explain each as a group.

    Open with a review of these approaches. Some participants will not have read the chapter and this will introduce them to the subject.

2. Which of the seven approaches have you heard people talk about the most? Which view do you lean toward yourself?

    Guide discussion with this two-pronged question, repeating the question before each one shares.

3. How could we introduce the more optimistic views to people in an authentic way?

    Wesleyan denominations have always tended to optimism about how much saving God can do in a person. Brainstorm the ways we can be more optimistic in encouraging others.

4. What are the four horizontal dynamics of holiness, which answer the question, "How saved can the world be?" List them as a group.

   Do a review of the four ways by inviting answers or looking them up in the chapter.

5. Which of the four dynamics of holiness are you most passionate about and what are you doing about it these days?

   Invite discussion and sharing that illustrates the various emphases of your participants. Follow up with reports on recent actions.

6. What other words for *sanctification* have you heard people use? Which do you like and dislike? Why?

   Lead a discussion of the other terms—even listing them on the board. You might find consensus or you might discover varied preferences on terminology. Seek understanding and thoughtful responses.

7. What Scriptures have you encountered that talk about holiness and help answer the questions, "How saved can you be?" and "How saved can the world be?"

   If the group can list some, invite them to offer them. They may refer to Scriptures like Leviticus 19:1–2; Deuteronomy 10:12; 30:6; Matthew 5:48; Mark 12:29–31; John 17:17–18; Romans 8:12–14; 12:1–2; 2 Corinthians 7:1; 13:9; Ephesians 5:17–18; 1 Thessalonians 4:3; 1 Peter 1:15–16; 1 John 3:2–3; and others. The Bible in both the Old and New Testaments seems to continually call God's followers to live obediently to God's commands and promises the power to do so.

8. What kind of preaching on sanctification did you hear years ago? What have you heard more recently?

    Invite older generations to share with younger people.

9. How does the general ethos of culture's pessimism or optimism affect what people believe about sanctification?

    Lead this important discussion of how the general pessimism of our culture works against the promise of purity from God. Invite popular quotes that Christians sometimes repeat that reinforce this pessimism (e.g.: "I'm not perfect, just forgiven" or "We all sin every day in thought, word, and deed").

10. When was the last time you heard a personal testimony about deliverance from a sin? Entire sanctification? Is there one you'd be willing to give now?

    Get many in the group to answer these questions. Invite someone to give their own testimony to being faithful to God and how this kind of life came to them. If nobody in your group can testify to receiving God's power to live obediently, see if there is someone in your church willing to testify. If there is nobody in your church with such a testimony, consider reading some of the testimonies from the last chapter in Holiness for Ordinary People *(twenty-fifth anniversary edition) by Keith Drury asking if these people were deceived or if they really experienced what they testified to. Close by having participants share what they learned today that brought them greater understanding of other views.*

8

Women in Leadership

1. Why do you think some churches and denominations refuse to
    ordain women?

    *Have the group make a list here. There is disagreement on
    ordination among Christian denominations. Catholics even
    refuse to ordain married men. Where do these stands come from
    and why are they taken?*

2. What advice would you give your daughter or granddaughter if
    she told you she was sure God was calling her into the ministry?

    *Be practical and get several answers to this question. Some may
    say, "Go for it—you must obey God!" Others may say, "You are
    deceived—God doesn't call women." Still others may say,
    "Marry a minister and be a preacher's wife." Keep the discussion
    practical at this point—what they'd actually say.*

3. Who are the women leaders in your own local church and what
    kind of role do they play?

    *Move the discussion from ordination to women in leadership. How
    is leadership different from ordained leadership? What about having*

women on your leadership board? What about a woman college president?

4. Who were the women leaders in the Bible that are models of female leadership?

   Have the group make a list. Use this time to discuss the role of women in ancient times and how much more difficult it would have been then for a woman leader.

5. List each of the standards for elders and ministers in Titus 1 and 1 Timothy 3, then ask how we use these standards for ministers today in our own church.

   List these on the board and discuss how we interpret them today. Especially note that the requirement of being "the husband of one wife" is not usually interpreted today as excluding single ministers or the obedient children requirement as excluding a minister without children.

6. What are some of the disadvantages a male minister has as a pastor? What are the disadvantages a female pastor has?

   List these for both genders—there are several.

7. What are some of the advantages a male minister has as a pastor? What are the advantages a female pastor has?

   List these for both genders—there are several.

8. What do we miss out on if all our preaching comes from males? What would we miss out on if all our preaching came from females?

In your listing as a group, you will probably discover that both genders have a particular perspective to offer in preaching. Keep the group from discussing preferences so much as content in preaching.

9. Some women pastors say they actually get more resistance from women in the church than from males. Why might this be true?

This is a very sensitive subject—it will help if people simply share what sometimes happens when husbands in the church respond to a woman preacher like their wives sometimes respond to male preachers. An open discussion with frank understanding may help everyone in your group.

10. How has the role of the preacher's wife changed over the years and how does this change relate to this discussion?

Older folk will be able to describe these changes and how they have influenced the role of women. Close by having participants share what they've learned today that brought them greater understanding of other views.

9

Denominational Leadership

1. Of the North American adult population, about 35 percent are in their twenties and thirties. What percent of attendees of our local church are in their twenties and thirties? Are we getting our share, or are they missing?

   Take time to work together and do the math on this question. That will be better than bringing the answer to the group. See if your church is missing its share of a generation or has more attendees in their twenties and thirties than the general population.

2. How many members of our own local church are in their twenties and thirties?

   Do the math together. Get the membership list and hand it out. Learning by actually doing the figuring will be more powerful than just hearing these numbers from a teacher.

3. What percent of our local church board are in their twenties and thirties?

   Do the math here too.

4. What might be the reasons our church differs from the general population? Why do we have so many (or so few) of this generation attending? Leading?

   Once the group has done the math for the first three questions, write the findings on the board. Then discuss why the numbers appear as they do.

5. What are the advantages to having some from the younger generation on the board in a local church? What are the risks or disadvantages?

   Make two lists—advantages and risks.

6. What are the three biggest barriers that keep younger generations from entering leadership service in our own church?

   Invite brainstorming and opinions, then lead the discussion to find consensus on the top three barriers.

7. Who are some of the younger folk in our church who would make good leaders?

   In this discussion, invite people to name names. This can be an affirming and sobering experience for young people.

8. What signs do older generations look for in younger folk that make them feel confident they are prepared to take leadership?

   The older generation may offer these best, though some younger folk may recognize the signs of maturity church members look for. Discuss which signs of maturity are best.

9. What ways do the older generations in a local church sponsor or mentor younger generations into future leadership? Who are the good examples of this kind of mentoring in your church now? Who are the best candidates for this kind of mentoring in the future?

   Brainstorm ideas for this kind of sponsoring; name names and make lists. Move the discussion toward action. Close by having participants share what they've learned today that brought them greater understanding of other views.

10

Ordained Ministry

1. How do you remember ministers being treated in the past compared to today? What have been good changes, and what do you think have been bad changes?

   Invite story-telling from older folk in the group. You will probably find the role and status of ministers has significantly changed over the years.

2. Do you feel called to your profession (speaking here to those who are not ordained ministers)? If so, how is your call different or similar to a minister's call?

   Discuss the call to ministry and the call to other professions and how your group sees them alike and different.

3. What are the advantages of having fifty-fifty representation of laity and ministers on all boards and committees above the local church in a denomination? Disadvantages? What other kinds of representation could we consider?

List the advantages together, and then imagine other ways of representation. Discuss how national values can influence church structures and representational requirements. Discuss church government and ask if there is one right way to do church government.

4. To what extent is the leveling value of many younger folk a good or bad value? What do you think of the trend of the last thirty years of centralization and increased authority for pastors and denominational leaders? What do you think the future holds: more of the same or a reversal of this trend?

Discuss both issues: leveling and centralization. Invite opinions and seek understanding. Is there a generational difference in your group or are differences a result of other factors?

5. Is there a way to raise the importance of lay life calling without reducing the importance of a ministerial calling? Or should the ministerial calling be emphasized less in the future? In recent years, how has the status or power of a minister increased or decreased?

Discuss the interplay of ministerial calling and lay life calling. Discuss practical evidence of how a minister's role is changing, evaluating the good and bad changes.

6. Who was called to ministry in the Bible? Were there people who entered the priesthood or ministry for a while, then left it later? Do you consider Luke a layman or a minister? What about the apostles? Phoebe? Barnabas? Pricilla?

Work through calling issues in the Bible by using the above names and others. Seek consensus wherever possible, but do not squelch differences in the process.

7. What exactly are we doing when we ordain a minister? Why do we ordain ministers? Why don't we ordain laity? Is the calling of a minister irrevocable and for a whole lifetime, or is it OK for a minister to leave ministry and start an insurance agency or enter some other profession at the age of fifty? When ministers retire, are they leaving the ministry? When a woman minister leaves the pastorate to raise her children for two decades, is that OK, or does she have to stay in pastoral work continually to be ordained?

Discuss these practical issues, which every district board faces. Make sure younger folk get their chance too; these are issues they will face even more in the future.

8. How does our church's size affect our view of the professional ministry? Lay leadership?

Discuss how the size of your church may affect how you view ministers. How might churches larger than yours see things differently? Smaller churches?

9. If you were designing the denomination on blank paper, how would you design ordination, the ministry, and the laity?

Do this mental game in order to find consensus and seek under-standing between the generations in how they see ministerial authority or even ministry itself. Close by having participants share what they've learned today that brought them greater understanding of other views.

Intergenerational Dialogue

1. What are the top five issues (in this book or beyond it) that the generations in your church still need to talk more about?

   Use your final session together to wrap up your intergenerational discussions, set some direction for the future, and affirm those who openly discussed and debated intergenerationally. Have each person list two to three issues that warrant more discussion between the generations—places to find greater consensus than you found in this group. Collect the list and read them one by one while somebody writes the tally on the board. After all items are listed, discuss and sort until you have the top five items for further discussion in the future.

2. What is the elephant-in-the-room issue in your church where the generations are still far apart? How can this conversation go on in order to carve out the future?

   Of all the items listed in number 1 above, which is the biggest one that needs more prayerful discussion. Where are the greatest differences? Brainstorm ways this discussion can go on in the future—maybe not right away, but someday soon.

3. Who are some of the good examples of people in your church who are great models of intergenerational listening and discussion? Who should we all try to be more like when talking with other generations?

    Use this time as positive affirmation of the best models in each generation—people who are examples of open and honest discussion. Open the discussion and have group members name names. However, keep this discussion from cannibalizing the answers to number 5 (which is more personal).

4. What kind of periodic format could be introduced where the generations come together for continuing discussions from time to time? Who would initiate that? How often? Where?

    Now, brainstorm ways this group (and perhaps others) could gather for this kind of intergenerational discussions in the future. If there is interest, see if you can nudge the discussion until someone volunteers to initiate it (or, better yet someone from each generation represented).

5. What person in another generation have you come to appreciate and admire more through these intergenerational discussions? What specifically do you appreciate about them?

    Close with an extremely personal and affirming activity as follows: Have each person reflect on the group experience and list one person they have especially come to appreciate, admire, and understand better. Have them write down a brief personal statement of admiration and affirmation—who is the person they have grown to appreciate more and why? Go around the group one by one with each person naming names. This final activity will be a tender time of affirmation and appreciation. Take your time and let the generations show their love and appreciation for each other. Then gather the entire group in a prayer huddle of two concentric circles. Have the younger generation face outward and lay their hands on the shoulders of the older folk and pray for them one by one. Then with the younger generation turned inward, have the older generation lay hands on them and pray for each—one by one—in a final prayer. Make sure you plan this well and leave plenty of time for this prayer meeting—it will probably be the highlight of the entire series of meetings.